Positive

the Power of
NO

how that little word you love to hate
can make or break your business

**Kim DeMotte
and
the Power of NO Team**

Facts on Demand Press
Tempe, Arizona

The Positive Power of NO
how that little word you love to hate can make or break your business

© 2003 Power of NO, LLC

Facts on Demand Press
PO Box 27869
Tempe, AZ 85285
(800) 929-3811

ISBN: 1-889150-40-1
Illustrations by: Dennis Fletcher
Photograph by: Suzy Gorman
Cover design by: Chris Scavotto
Inside layout by: Ad Graphics, Inc.

DeMotte, Kim.
   The positive power of no : how that little word you
love to hate can make or break your business / Kim
DeMotte and the Power of NO Team.
      p. cm.
      Includes index.
      ISBN 1-889150-40-1

   1. Management. 2. Decision making. I. Power of NO
(Firm) II. Title.

   HD31.D4224 2003   658.4
                      QBI03-200265

PREFACE

A mentor of mine, Kent Ekstrom, drifted into my world quite serendipitously in 1995 for the express purpose of teaching me the Positive Power of NO. He didn't realize that was his mission, but that's what he accomplished. Kent was (and still is) a master at building prospecting foundations for sales processes from helping his customers decide what it is they do to scripting prospecting specialists to hiring and training people who spend their days sifting through potential buyers. It was like a light bulb over my head.

In 1997 and 1998 I shared with Dr. Lynn Walker a tremendously rewarding consulting experience in the Major Gift and Planned Giving organization for one of the nation's largest 501c(3) foundations. Dr. Walker, a prominent management psychologist, and I had the occasionally frustrating but often inspiring task of helping these folks decide what they were NOT as well as what they WERE, who their fundraising prospects WERE and who they were NOT. On went another light bulb over my head.

From 1998 to the present, I have become increasingly aware of how much better off my clients would be (from sole proprietors to small, family owned businesses to Fortune 1000 behemoths) if they just could learn why, when, where, and how to say NO when it defended and supported their strategic planning. So many businesses have been dragged over the edge of success and out of the ring by an inability to focus on what they do best; by hiring friends and referrals for critical positions without adequate assessment; and by depreciating their work force with outdated management/leadership rules. More and more it became evident I had a mission: to evangelize the Power of NO.

As I shared these ideas, this concept – that NO was not a four-letter word, and that NO could solve a myriad of business problems – seemed to resonate with fellow consultants within my sphere. In January of

2001 I entertained a houseful of these consultants and this book was conceived. I have had unwavering support from friends and associates who watched from the sidelines as this project took shape. I can't thank my assistant Maureen Gelzer enough for cleaning up after me and keeping this adventurous Senior Citizen headed in the right direction. Ever responsive editor, Dave Nicklaus dutifully cleaned up chapter after chapter allowing all the authors' individuality to still shine through. And of course family. My Mom and Dad don't have a clue what I do, but they want me to do it right! My wife, Margaret, has lived and breathed this project for the past 16 months even while completing her MBA. My two daughters, Rebecca and Mindy, one on the west coast and one on the east, called diligently every Sunday night for status reports and sanity checks. And Bubba, Gabby, Dillinger and J. Edgar (Lab, Border Collie, Cat, Cat) curled up at my feet or on my lap (depending on species) late at night while I pored over chapters. Thank you all.

It has dawned on me that not everybody is ready for this message. This entire tome may be a "NO" for you. That's OK. It's an indication that you already have some idea of how to use NO. You're on the right track. But if there's one idea, one speck of wisdom, one story that makes you wake up at night thinking about managing a process better, focusing more clearly, or committing to saying NO to just one thing that harms your bottom line, keep the book on your shelf. Make it available to your friends. Pass it around your office. Share it. Help me evangelize the Positive Power of NO.

Kim DeMotte
St. Louis, Missouri
April, 2003

TABLE OF CONTENTS

WHAT IF HE HAD JUST SAID NO?

CHAPTER I

A Primer on NO: Why, When, Where and How to Say NO

Kim DeMotte

WHY?

Without a "why" we have no reason to do anything.

> "If I had a hammer, I'd hammer in the morning. I'd hammer in the evening, all over this land."
>
> "I'd hammer out danger. I'd hammer out a warning. I'd hammer out love between my brothers and my sisters all over this land."
>
> *(music and lyrics by Lee Hays and Pete Seeger, 1958)* [i]

OK, so I'm dating myself. But "If I Had a Hammer" led an entire generation to believe that they could fix almost anything if they hammered away at it. We were told that we could do, have or be anything. There were no limits; overachieving was expected. Most of us eventually realized there were limits. The question was, who established them? Was I going to be excluded or included from some activity, sport, girlfriend or boyfriend because society said so, or because I said so? Who drew the limits? Was it fair for our parents to tell us there were no limits when we knew there were? No wonder therapists are thriving!

If there were a tool – like Pete Seeger's hammer – that could repair any management or organizational crisis, and even do preventive maintenance to avoid the crisis in the first place, how much would you pay for it? What would it be worth to be able to reduce stress, solve communications problems, avoid mistakes, shore up disintegrating profits, improve the output of a low-producing workforce, hire exactly the right employee, and much, much more?

Furthermore, what if this tool could work its magic regardless of a changing environment? What if this tool was created from the simplest materials, but didn't come with a set of operating instructions? Would it be worthwhile to learn, by trial and error if necessary, how to effectively use this tool to improve your life, family, and business?

The tool I'm speaking about is the word "NO." Used without prejudice to defend our individual core values or corporate strategy, the word NO is the most effective tool you can use to take control of any situation.

Let me share some examples of people who wielded this tool skillfully, shouting NO from the rooftops to improve a life, a company, and a country.

The young patriot strode to the podium, the last to speak to a tired audience. I have paraphrased the speech to focus on key points:

"....It is natural to man to indulge in the illusions of hope. We are apt to shut our eyes against a painful truth, and listen to the song of that siren till she transforms us into beasts .... Are we disposed to be of the number of those who, having eyes, see not, and having ears, hear not, the things which so nearly concern their temporal salvation? For my part, whatever anguish of spirit it may cost, I am willing to know the whole truth; to know the worst, and to provide for it ....

...I have but one lamp by which my feet are guided, and that is the lamp of experience. I know of no way of judging of the future but by the past...

If we wish to be free – if we mean to preserve inviolate those inestimable privileges for which we have been so long contending ... we must fight! I repeat it, sir, we must fight! ...

 They tell us, sir, that we are weak; unable to cope with so formidable an adversary. But when shall we be stronger? Will it be the next week, or the next year? ... Shall we gather strength by irresolution and inaction?

The battle, sir, is not to the strong alone; it is to the vigilant, the active, the brave.

The war is inevitable – and let it come! I repeat it, sir, let it come.

I know not what course others may take but as for me: Give me liberty or give me death!"

(Excerpted from a speech delivered by Patrick Henry) [ii]

The subject of this famous oration is, of course, the struggle for freedom from a rule of law that was not in the common citizen's best interest in 1775. American colonists were being taxed without representation, disarmed and told how to practice religion. Yet, until patriots such as Patrick Henry spurred the colonists to action, they were relying on hope alone to solve the problem. Do we do that in our businesses? Do we postpone the inevitable in order to maintain calm in our organizations? Do we ignore history and hope it won't happen again? Do we feel *"weak; unable to cope with so formidable an adversary?"* In our world, how does that adversary manifest itself? Is it the underperforming employee we cannot seem to release? The unprofitable customer demand we cannot deny? The constant change that seems to rip our calm productive fabric daily? Is it corporate Attention Deficit Disorder that tells us to try everything and see what works?

In business, we must be *"willing to know the whole truth; to know the worst, and to provide for it."* We must accept a call to action so that we may *"preserve inviolate those inestimable privileges for which we have been so long contending"* [iii] – privileges such as an acceptable profit, a good work environment, productive employees and healthy, happy families. It all depends on you, citizen soldier.

What part of your business is under siege? What part of your life is bound by chains of habit, culture, always-been-done-that-way? When will you reach the limits of toleration and declare NO. I'm not doing that again. I'm not giving in. That's not who I am. That violates my most basic values. That's simply not in my best interests. My organization won't survive.

"NO is the Foundation of Free Will"

In 1980, Roberta Guaspari's world came apart.

The mother of three and wife of a naval officer found herself smack in the middle of her husband's midlife crisis and a divorce. As a Navy wife, she had never worked for a living, but she had finished college at the State

University of New York and earned a master's degree in music education at Boston University. There must be something she could do, but she had to do it in a hurry. After the divorce there was nothing for her or her two sons. She decided to teach the subject she loved, music. But where? Where was she needed? This proper, white, middle-class Italian girl with a master's degree took a job in East Harlem, N.Y. She proposed to teach, of all things, the violin. There was little money for a teacher and absolutely no money for instruments. If she wanted to teach these children, she would have to show up with her own violins! And she did.

Music was her passion. Tough love was her method. She was a stern taskmaster, something her charges had rarely if ever experienced. She didn't have the resources to coddle these students; she didn't even have the resources to coddle herself or her own children. She had her limits on behavior, commitment and performance and she made them known. The children who took her classes were expected to pay attention, practice and perform within her expectations. Does that sound like a novel idea? It was so novel that after several months, parents came to the school administration and demanded that she back off. She was too tough on the East Harlem kids. They couldn't deal with all this accountability. The school administration ordered her to stretch her limits, her core beliefs, and begin to accept whatever her students brought her. Whatever they did was to be deemed acceptable. She was sick over it. But she would not abandon her students, so she went into the classroom a different teacher.

The students noticed immediately. They would challenge her with mediocre performance or lowered practice standards and wait for the barrage of NO. When it didn't come, the students became curious, even suspicious. They had grown to clearly understand Roberta Guaspari's limits and the NOes that occurred when those limits were crossed. They missed them. They felt adrift, with no direction. They were uncomfortable. Her students petitioned the administration to allow her to teach the "old way." They bolstered in her the courage to hold her course. The administration's demands had forced her to violate her own personal limits. She was coached by her own students to say NO to these demands and begin applying her limits once again.

From that point, the story is legendary. You may know it from the short film "Small Wonders" or the feature-length Wes Craven movie, "Music of the Heart," starring Meryl Streep as Roberta. Her students played (and still play) Carnegie Hall at the invitation of such luminaries as Itzhak Perlman and Isaac Stern. Today her classes are filled through a lottery system. Only 50 percent of the students wanting to learn from her are accepted. Even as many parts of this nation turned their backs on music education during the 1990s, this one bright light shone through.[iv]

"NO is the Cornerstone of Character"

The young actor, starving by most standards, and selling 80-cent meals at a small Harlem restaurant, reviewed a script from an agent he did not know. He was incredibly excited, because it represented his first serious work possibility in over a year. This part would mean $750 a week – a fortune in 1950.

He read the script and didn't like it. He was being offered the role of a man who had witnessed a murder. In the script, the bad guys would stop at nothing to keep the witness silent, including dumping his young daughter's body on his front lawn. The character was enraged, but could not bring himself to act on his own behalf. He remained passive, allowing others to fight his battles for him.

After reading the script, Sidney Poitier told agent Marty Baum he was not going to play the part. Knowing what this could mean to Poitier financially, Baum was dumbstruck. The part was not racially derogatory. The script did not include name-calling or any other debasing relationship. Poitier could not tell Baum why at the time, but he knew he had to pass up this role.

I thanked him and left. Then I went over to 57th Street and Broadway, one flight up, to a place called Household Finance Company, and I borrowed seventy-five dollars on the furniture in our apartment, because I needed the money. The birth of our second daughter was fairly near, and I knew Beth Israel Hospital was going to cost me seventy-five bucks so I had to line up the money.

Sidney Poitier [v]

Sidney Poitier had left his home in the Bahamas as a boy of 15, and had survived on his own for eight years. One more delay in the success he knew he would have would not make him compromise his ideals, even under terrible financial strain. Six months later, when Baum signed as Poitier's agent and launched his career, Poitier told Baum he had rejected the part because *"the character didn't measure up. He didn't fight for what mattered to him most. He didn't behave with dignity."*[vi]

When was the last time you sold out? Knew what it felt like to drop your prices in order to stay busy? Took on a job that was not your forte' because you "needed the gig?" Agreed to work late when your son's baseball team was playing for a title? Failed to reject a proposal you just knew you'd regret? Hired the next applicant rather than press the interview process to its limits? How did you feel about that?

"NO is the Icon of Integrity"

NO is the foundation of free will, the cornerstone of character and the icon of integrity. The free will defended by Patrick Henry, the character of Roberta Guaspari and the integrity of Sidney Poitier bolster the fortitude necessary to once again learn the use of the word NO to improve our lives. Why not manage your organization with these attributes?

Presidents have used NO when their citizens' lives were on the line (JFK in the Cuban Missile Crisis; Lincoln in the Civil War). When King Edward VIII of England gave up his throne to marry the divorced Mrs. Simpson, he was saying NO to violations of his privacy and to unacceptable limits on his personal life. When Cmdr. James Stockdale (who later became Ross Perot's 1992 vice presidential running mate) was a prisoner of war in North Vietnam, he said NO to his captors' inhumane demands in the most extreme way possible: by attempting suicide. His courage secured better treatment for his fellow prisoners.

NO is the substance of which personal, corporate and national victory is born. It can be your substance too.

So if it is so powerful, why is it so hard?

Robert Cialdini tells us in his book *Influence: The Psychology of Persuasion*, that six weapons of influence are working on us at all times to get us to do things, buy things, say things, go along with things.[vii] Cialdini uses these weapons as teaching aids in his education of marketers. He's in the BUSINESS of teaching others how to make certain you do not say NO! That's his job. But it's our job to defend ourselves!

So here you are. You're twenty-something, thirty-something or fifty-something and you have a hard time saying NO. Maybe now you understand why. It's a conspiracy and you've been trained since birth that NO is not an effective word. You hate to have it said to you. And highly paid professionals are working to keep you from saying NO. The deck is stacked against you. *IT'S NOT YOUR FAULT!* There. I said it! It's not your fault. But it IS your fault if you don't take charge of your business and your life by learning why, when, where and how to say NO.

For two decades, management and personal-development gurus have been telling us to focus on our goal, our mission, our vision or our dream. "Creative visualization" is supposed to help us focus energy and resources on what we want. Maybe you've been in a meeting where someone taped flip chart page after flip chart page on the walls of strategic planning purgatory to help all the team members internalize where the organization is going, and what it is and what it will be. Without a map, you can't get anywhere. Without a plan, you're rudderless. But, WAIT! What defines that goal, that mission, that vision, that dream? It's defined best by what you'll say NO to in order to achieve it! The NOes define the YESes!

Jerry Harvey in his management tome *The Abilene Paradox*, defines what happens when we can't bring ourselves to say NO.[viii] Harvey tells the story of a family that decides, on a terribly hot day in West Texas, to drive 53 miles to Abilene for a meal. Their car has no air-conditioning, and when they return home bedraggled, sweaty, and generally miserable, they make a startling discovery. Each family member had acquiesced to the trip because he or she thought it was what the group wanted. In fact, no one wanted to make the trip, but make the trip they did. No one said no.

Harvey also offers a more serious example of the consequences of failing to say NO. Jeb Magruder, convicted as a co-conspirator in the aftermath of the 1972 Watergate break-in, later confided to Senator Howard Baker, "I am sure that if I had fought vigorously against it, I think any of us could have had the plan cancelled."[ix] Do things just 'go through' in your organization because no one knows how to say "NO"? Does the culture of your management leave the potential heroes of your business silent? Would you like to pull the plug on some research, marketing, hiring or expansion plan that you just *know* does not support the strategic direction of your organization? You need to find out.

That's why.

WHEN?

When should you be prepared to say NO? Ideally, you should say NO whenever a predetermined limit has been breached. The word "predetermined" is important. It says you've thought about it and you're not reacting on the fly. It implies that there should be some planning. The behavioral and performance limits Roberta Guaspari applied to her students were not easy, but they were necessary. When she withdrew them under pressure, her musicians were rudderless and lost. If you don't understand the negative impact of some proposals you've accepted in the past, any limits you set going forward will be arbitrary. Remember Patrick Henry's comment: *"...I have but one lamp by which my feet are guided, and that is the lamp of experience. I know of no way of judging of the future but by the past."*[x] Our past should give us the parameters with which to control our future, set our limits and say NO when those limits are breached. As soon as you realize that the proposal's outside your limits or that the applicant is flawed, pull the trigger and say NO. Doing anything else borders on dishonesty. If you know an applicant is not suited for the job and you don't end the interview, you're giving rise to false hope, followed by disappointment and, if nothing else, wasted interview time. Preparing proposals for bids for which you know you're not a fit is using resources for the sake of using resources. NO is the answer. It's going to be the answer tomorrow or next week anyway, why not now?

WHERE?

The best 'place' to say NO is in the other person's space. What do I mean by that? If you've concluded that the proposal is outside the limits, and for you it's a NO, then *now* is the appropriate time to say it, and you should take your NO *to* the rejected party. Waiting for him or her to call you is fraught with miscommunication, false hope, and listening problems ("you didn't tell me NO, so I assumed 'YES'"). Sometimes, when you know that your NO is going to be a problem for the other party, you may need to go out of your way to deliver the news. Notice I didn't say "the bad news." NO is not automatically bad news. NO ends the current negotiation so both parties can get on with their investigations. Delayed, wishy-washy, ill-communicated "maybes" keep both parties in suspended animation like a doe caught in the headlights. It's symbolic of a slow death! YOU'RE IN CHARGE! If it's a NO for you then it's a NO. Take it to them so both of you can move on.

How?

To demonstrate how limits work, let's use an illustration. We call this an **Ideal Target** (See inside front cover). In archery, the most valuable spot on the target is the point that is dead center. If your arrow strikes that spot, you receive the maximum score. If your arrow lands away from the center, it receives a lower score. If you're too far away, your score is zero. The yellow bull's-eye defines an acceptable level of deviation from the center where you still receive the maximum score. Skill-wise, an arrow a little off center isn't as good as one dead center, but it's counted as a bull's-eye as long as it lands in the yellow circle.

Not until your arrow strikes the red ring around the yellow circle does your score actually diminish. Imagine you're competing with someone who has shot nine consecutive bull's-eyes and a red ring. You've shot nine consecutive bull's-eyes with one shot left. What do you have to do on your tenth to win? Of course, you have to hit another bull's-eye. It's important. It's just as important that your organization do on-target things every day. Hire bull's-eye employees. Acquire bull's-eye business. Expand into bull's-eye markets. Manufacture bull's-eye products and offer bull's-eye services.

But what defines the bull's-eye? The red ring around it defines the limits. If you hit anything but that yellow circle, you *do not win*. Yellow is a YES. Red is a NO. On the **Ideal Target**, yellow is the goal and red is not supportive of the goal. The limit is refined, and discriminating. The bull's-eye makes up a small, select portion of the target.

Sometimes the targets (goals, mission, vision, dream) in our personal and business lives look more like an **Anything Goes Target**. Even a not-very-accurate shot counts as a bull's-eye. The red ring (which defines the bull's-eye) is stretched so far as to allow almost anything that hits the target to be counted as a bull's-eye, even if it's nowhere near the center. Is this your situation? Is everything a YES for you? Is your business attempting to be all things to all people? Do you find yourself saying YES to things that are nowhere near the center of your vision? Does your sales force concede pricing issues? Are you losing the customer satisfaction vs. profitability war? Are you pressured to take on volunteer responsibilities that compromise time with your family and friends? The **Anything Goes Target** shows up frequently in our hurried, hassled, trying-to-please-everybody lives. It is a target with clear limits between YES and NO, but the limits are so loosely bound as to make a YES possible for almost any proposition. Be aware of it. Be VERY aware of it. Eliminating this model is the reason you'll want to finish this book!

The first step to using the Positive Power of NO is to identify your red ring. Since your goals, aspirations, vision and mission are yours to create, so, too, are the limits that surround them. If your goals are represented by the yellow bull's-eye, then the red ring (which really defines the bull's-eye) is your choice as well. Knowing what is NOT your goal, what does NOT support your strategic vision, who is NOT right for a particular position and what volunteer post will NOT support your picture of happiness is the secret to focusing your energies on what you really want in life, and what you and your business will be. The NOes define the YESes. What you are NOT and will NOT do defines what you ARE and what you WILL do.

> **The Positive Power of NO is the advantage you get when you're as clear about what you DON'T want as you are about what you WANT.**

We use a tool called Limit Theory™ to describe what happens when an organization moves from wide open, unlimited, "everything for everybody" management to Power of NO management. Limit Theory™

holds that the clearer the boundary between acceptable and unacceptable, between YES and NO, the more successful the outcome of any management exercise.

Michael Porter, the noted Harvard Business School professor, has stated: *"A strategy delineates a territory in which a company seeks to be unique. Strategy 101 is about choices. You can't be all things to all people."* He goes on to say, *"The essence of strategy is that you must set limits on what you're tying to accomplish. The company without a strategy is willing to do anything."*[xi]

Further, management research author Jim Collins in his book *Good to Great* found one of the key parameters that made good companies great was *"The good-to-great companies did not focus on what to do to become great; they focused equally on what not do to and what to stop doing."*[xii] Can you see the red ring here?

For all the aforementioned reasons, we struggle to tell ourselves (and our supporters, employees, confidants, etc.) what's a NO in our world. If we're fortunate enough to be able to say what we WANT, it's rare that we have given thought to what we DON'T want. To take advantage of the Power of NO, we need be able to say, "This is what we DON'T want" as well as, "This is what we want." But when we begin to take control of our NOes, our target looks like the **Big Fuzzy Target**. We can conceive of some proposal, way out on the fringes of yellow-red, as unacceptable. But as we move closer to the center, it gets more acceptable. So somewhere out toward the edges is a NO, and as our accuracy moves toward the center it becomes a YES.

But how do we teach this to our employees, our volunteers and our kids? How would you feel if your boss accepted an arrow four inches from the center (kind of reddish-yellow), but criticized you for an arrow three inches from the center (more yellowish-red)? This typically manifests itself in a statement that "bosses don't need to follow the rules." For example, an executive might "wrap up a deal" his salesperson couldn't by exceeding the acceptable limits of the company, compromising on pricing, quality or delivery. Or a management team might set operational policy limits in a strategic planning session, and then discipline an employee who takes the directive literally. To make Limit Theory™ work in your organization, you must keep the boundary *crystal clear* between Yellow and Red, between acceptable and unacceptable, between YES and NO. These boundaries must be supported from the highest levels of management down. From an employee's point of view, the **Anything Goes Target** is much easier to live with. It says "anything's OK." But the **Big Fuzzy Target** says "almost anything *might* be OK." The **Anything Goes Target** is good for the employee. At least he knows that most of what he does will be accepted. But it's terrible for the company. It says, "We'll do anything for anybody to make a buck." "We'll hire anybody to fill that vacancy." "We will not spend the resources to focus our efforts by thoughtfully explaining what's NOT wanted." An **Anything Goes Target** is what you find in an organization with a *laissez faire* management style. It yields happy employees and struggling stockholders/stakeholders.

The **Big Fuzzy Target** is typically found in an organization where management has one eye on the bottom line and the other on its image in the marketplace, and vacillates back and forth on which is more important in any given circumstance. The target shows quite succinctly that the leadership has provided no clear boundaries between acceptable and unacceptable. Depending on whom the client knows, a lower price *might* be accepted. Depending on who interviews a potential employee, and on what day, and what mood the interviewer is in, the applicant *might* be hired on the spot. Depending on the month's financial situation, we *might* take on this piece of business that's really not our specialty. Strategic planning be damned!

So how do we move our organization, and our lives, away from being everything to everybody? How can we gain control over situations without slamming our train into a brick wall? It is a three-step process. Our goal, symbolically, is to define an **Ideal Target** with a crystal clear, appropriately sized yellow bull's-eye (acceptable) surrounded by a sharply drawn red ring (unacceptable).

Step one. Move your organization from the **Anything Goes Target** to the **Big Fuzzy Target**. The culture will begin to understand that something at the outer limits is less desirable than the inner areas of the target. This step can be taken in any area of your organization, such as human resources, finance, sales or production. At the outermost edges of the center circle, the color is red. That's a NO. Your employees will feel somewhat restricted by the shrinking acceptability of off-target behavior, but you have taken the first step.

Step two. Decisively shrink the blue circle (which, of course, defines the red-yellow fuzzy circle in a **Big Fuzzy Target**), thus slowly constricting the number of bad proposals accepted, wrong people hired, unprofitable product manufactured, etc. This will create what we call a **Better Fuzzy Target**. A **Better Fuzzy Target** still has issues with forming a crystal clear boundary between Yellow and Red, between YES and NO, but has at least set some clear limits beyond which NO is absolutely the answer. Compared with a **Big Fuzzy Target**, the world of "possibly acceptable" is substantially reduced.

Step three. Make the boundary between the yellow bull's-eye and the red ring *crystal clear*. This brings your organization back to an **Ideal Target**. Isn't that what you set out to accomplish in your strategic planning? Isn't that your goal/mission/vision/dream in the first place? When everyone in your organization knows what you *are* and what you *are not*; what you *will* do and what you *will not* do, your organization has defined itself and clearly is operating in a manner consistent with Michael Porter's notion. Remember, *"The essence of strategy is that you must set limits on what you're tying to accomplish."*[xiii]

<u>Do not underestimate the struggle involved in these three steps.</u> Engaging in the corporate or individual exercise of setting limits and learning to prosper within those limits is fraught with roadblocks. There are always the occasional limit-breaking exercises that turn out to be serendipitously positive. CAUTION! That's a classical definition of a superstition. Mighty Casey wore green socks on the day he hit three home runs, so he changes his daily behavior and wears green socks forever. We also must overcome a lifetime of trained responses to situations. After all, we've had a hard time with this NO stuff since we were kids! But you *can* teach an old dog new tricks. You just need to be patient, consistent and persistent.

Do not use these limits as excuses to reject everything, or discriminate in any unethical or illegal manner. On occasion we have all met someone whose view of the world is so limited as to reject almost everything. The **Anal Target**, makes an acceptable shot all but impossible. As in any adjustable system, one can go too far. The boss whose initial response to every idea is NO is not constructive. The company that builds policy based on discriminating against a legally protected class (race, religion, gender, etc.) is headed for litigation. The company that builds policy based on unethical limits (tolerating sexual harassment or manipulating pay grades, for example) won't survive in the long run.

> **NO is the Foundation of Free Will, the Cornerstone of Character and the Icon of Integrity.**
>
> **The Positive Power of NO is the advantage you get when you're as clear about what you DON'T want as you are about what you WANT.**

To repeat it succinctly, the NOes define the YESes. What we are is often defined by what we are NOT. The popular behavior assessment tool DISC helps us determine our predictable behavior patterns by asking two series of questions.[xiv] Half are asked in the vein of what we are MOST like, and the other half in the vein of what we are LEAST like. The responses to the first (MOST like) determine our predictable behavior patterns in our external (working, socializing, etc.) world. But the responses to the set of questions asking what we are LEAST like determine the behavior patterns we are *naturally endowed with*. They show who we are when we are ourselves in our natural habitat. DISC defines us most naturally by what we are NOT.

The preceding philosophies and stories are purposefully symbolic. They are meant to give the reader a framework on which to hang practical applications. In the following chapters we will show you how to improve outcomes from the various processes that you use to run your organizations and your lives.

You too can manage your life and your company (and we know for some of you there is very little difference) with the free will and determination of a Patrick Henry, the character of a Roberta Guaspari and the integrity of a Sidney Poitier. Shrink the red ring. Make the limits razor sharp so you and your team members will have no doubt about where YES becomes NO. Develop the fortitude to reject proposals, applicants, products, customers, vendors or standard operating procedures that fall ever so slightly outside those limits.

How do you say NO? This is perhaps the most difficult part of the process to coach. Always say NO with compassion and dignity. Always say it in a spirit of "this didn't work out, but I wanted you to know as soon as possible because you have a problem to resolve and I don't have the answer." An exception to this might be in a bid response to a blind Request For Proposal (RFP) (from a company with which you have no prior relationship, or do not intend to have one in the future. In this case, you need make no response at all. Base your response on the future potential of the RFP prospect.)

Let's remember the reason for saying "NO." NO is the Foundation of Free Will, the Cornerstone of Character and the Icon of Integrity. It is not the Domain of Dragging On, the Mark of Maybe or the Signature of Stress! We owe it to ourselves to get on with it! Roberta Guaspari did not let her students get by with disruptive behavior, shoddy performance or mediocre commitment. Sidney Poitier did not let his agent-to-be think that he would take any role for a crack at stardom. And Patrick Henry implored "The battle, sir, is not to the strong alone; it is to the vigilant, the active, the brave. The war is inevitable – and let it come! I repeat it, sir, let it come." [xv] There was nothing wimpy about the way these three said NO. Their limits had been breached. They held their heads high, faced their opponents and rejected the status quo. You can, and you must, train yourself to do the same.

Caveat: Every exception to your limit becomes a reason to except yet again. If you must violate your rule, then rewrite the limit! But take the time and effort to do it *on purpose*. Do not change the limits based on external pressures. Do not change the limits on a whim, or to get one more order, or to fill one more position. When it's time to change the limits, do so with forethought and logic that will serve your strategic goals. Your organization will run smoother, more profitably, with less stress and better decision making at all levels.

An integral part of the Power of NO is the concept that everything is NOT a fit for *everything else*! We understand that your organization may be running as smoothly as you could imagine. You may already be using the principles outlined above. If so, *congratulations*. If it's blind luck, *congratulations* on that, too. But perhaps you're *not* perfectly satisfied with various processes in your organization and you turned here for help.

If you choose to jump in, you will learn why, when, where and how to say NO to things that stray you from your goal, your mission, your vision, your dream. You will learn how to set limits and put constraints on the processes that run amok in your world. You will learn how to think as much about what you DON'T want as about what you WANT, about what you will NOT do as about what you WILL do, and about who you are NOT as much as who you ARE. You will learn the tools that make it easier to sleep at night knowing that you are a leader of free will, character and integrity.

ONE MORE THING....

OK. Let's presume that you get it. CONGRATULATIONS! I implore you not to be a hypocrite! As the Gnome of NO, the Rajah of Rejection, the King of Killing It, you have a responsibility to teach others. It will dawn on you at some point that, in your environment, you are unique in this matter. You've set limits and said NO to all the right things. You have control of your organization and your life. But others still have problems saying NO. And guess what? Their inability to say NO can wreak as much havoc on your life as your own. When they said, "I'll try" to your request of some volunteer job at your church, you might have foolishly assumed that they'd actually show up! As a matter of fact, you accepted that "I'll try" to convince yourself you didn't need to make any more calls, because you had the job filled. Face it. If they knew how, they would have told you NO. But alas, they are not so equipped. To avoid these frustrations, it's up to you to help them say NO. What, you cry? I WANT them to volunteer. Why would I help them reject my request? Because you'd rather know RIGHT NOW that they had no intention of helping instead of being frustrated with their "no-show" later. Responses like "I'll try," "Send me some literature," and "Let's see what happens" are typical from people who do not possess the understanding you've gained in the last 20 pages or so. To further reduce the stress in your life, help them say NO when they need to. Find another volunteer. Call another prospect. See another applicant. When you help THEM move on, YOU can move on.

As we've seen, NO can work miracles. Ask any American historian, Sidney Poitier's many fans or Roberta Guaspari's students. Ask yourself. Yes, ask yourself.

The philosophies underscored above can improve organizations, companies and relationships, but they have to be followed by one person at a time. Choose to use the Positive Power of NO. It's a very personal undertaking. It's entirely up to you.

*   *   *   *   *   *   *

i   Words and music by Lee Hays and Pete Seeger, 1958.

ii   Excerpted from a speech delivered by Patrick Henry (1736-1799) before the Second Virginia Convention on March 23, 1775 at St. John's Episcopal Church in Richmond.

iii Ibid.

iv   Guaspari, Roberta with Larkin Warren, *Music of the Heart* (Hyperion: New York, 1999). Small Wonders (Fiddlefest) directed by Allen Miller and produced by Susan Kaplan, Documentary Music of the Heart directed by Wes Craven, Miramax Films, 1999.

v   Poitier, Sidney, *The Measure of a Man: a Spiritual Biography*, (Harper: San Francisco, 2000).

vi   Ibid.

vii Cialdini, Robert B. PhD. Influence, The Psychology of Persuasion, (William Morrow and Company: New York, 1984).

viii Harvey, Jerry B., *The Abilene Paradox and Other Meditations on Management* (Jossey-Bass: San Francisco: 1988). The original publication of the Abilene Paradox appeared as: "The Abilene Paradox: The Management of Agreement," in *Organizational Dynamics* (Summer 1974).

ix   Ibid.

x   Henry, 1775.

xi   Hammonds, Keith. "Michael Porter's Big Ideas," Fast Company, March 2001.

xii Collins, Jim. *Good to Great: Why Some Companies Make the Leap and Others Don't*, (Harper Collins Publishers: New York, 2001)

xiii Hammonds, 2001.

xiv The DISC model is based on the work of William Moulton Marston. For more details, see "DISC: The Universal Language," a reference manual by Bill J. Bonnstetter, Judy Suiter, & Randy Widrick published by Target Training International, Ltd.

xv   Henry, 1775.

ABOUT THE AUTHORS

The authors of this book have amassed more than 200 years of business experience.

Unlike typical "anthology" authors, who contribute their isolated stories or vignettes and may not even know one another, every member of the Power of NO team lives in St. Louis. They often work shoulder-to-shoulder with mutual clients. They interact with each other on a daily basis, and their contributions to this project are just as closely intertwined.

They come from the entrepreneurial world. They've experienced Fortune 100 battles. They come from the family business environment and have survived non-profit debacles. They have worked as team players in multiple scenarios and as independents in others.

You won't find any hyper-theoretical academicians on our list, although several members of the group hold advanced degrees. You won't find practitioners who make their living primarily on the speaking circuit, although several are professional members of the National Speakers Association.

Every member of the Power of NO team is a "rubber-meets-the-road" practitioner of his or her specific expertise. Working and honing their skills is a daily exercise. And they took the time to put their collective wisdom on paper for you.

CHAPTER II.

NO Thyself: Individual Strategies for Thinking and Choosing

What the Delphic Oracle might say today.[i]

Sarah Bassett

First, a warning: If you're looking for an off-the-shelf template that will do it all for you – turn around your business, make more money, determine what direction to take – then you might be disappointed. *The Positive Power of No* isn't a set of preprogrammed remedial steps. It isn't a diagnostic tool designed to yield The Answer. This isn't about imposing a new system onto your business – in other words, trying to change it from the outside in.

Rather, what we're talking about is a change that comes from the inside out. It all starts, ends and lives with you, the individual.

The Power of NO describes a way of thinking clearly that results in strong choices and wholehearted commitment. For it to work – really work, and not just give the appearance of working – ideally every individual in your organization should understand the value of NO. It isn't ordered from on high ("you must think this way so that you get the results upper management wants") or artificially scripted into an organization's vocabulary (calling what you're already doing "limit theory," for instance, when it's really the same-old, same-old). It's much more than a cosmetic change: It *registers* within each individual.

This is what releases NO's power.

To put it another way, the Power of NO hinges on your own understanding of how we human beings are made. Inspired by a simple, universal principle, the Power of NO begins, ends and resides in the individual human psyche.

Here's the principle:

> **You become empowered when you're as clear about what you DON'T want as you are about what you WANT.**

We're talking about something innate, but something many of us have lost sight of. We want to make this principle conscious, help you remember it and then delineate the many ways you can use it. We're presenting for your consideration a simple, powerful, even obvious strategy which is already an integral part of our psychological makeup, but which we've devalued, forgotten or simply overlooked. Each individual needs to enlighten himself or herself as to why, when, where, and how to say NO; it doesn't work nearly as well if you try to distill NO into a set of rules or commandments.

You can use something as natural as NO to jump-start your business, career, relationships, private life and more. And we're asserting that no matter how conscientiously you try to use the NO system in all these domains, it has to resonate first in the individual. If it doesn't, if you can't see how it's already at work in us all, then the results won't be optimal, no matter how much a boss insists that people have to use NO when selling or managing or strategizing.

Because the Power of NO is first and foremost an individual process. It's already part of you.

A NO-BRAINER

At some level we already comprehend the fundamental principle embodied in NO or at least sense it operating in our lives. It's woven into the fabric of our individual psyches. But for one reason or another, we've forgotten, rejected or been trained out of it.

When you were a kid, chances are you were already employing the Power of NO. During the terrible twos, NO helped you delineate the difference between you and other, you and environment, your desires vs. someone else's. In your teenage years, NO was a declaration of burgeoning independence and individuality. You employed the principle instinctively.

Since then you've been educated out of your natural tendency. We were probably halted in our tracks by that word between 17,000 and 21,000 times in our early youth. NO is not polite, you learned. It's not politic. It makes people dislike you. It loses business. It's bitchy. It cuts through to the heart of an issue so you have to take a stand, which means less wiggle room. It sounds unpleasant. It's (gasp!) *negative*.

Better to say yes to your customers, your friends, your co-workers, your constituents and certainly your boss, right? That way, everyone will like you. All doors will open for you. You and your business will thrive.

This way of thinking, then, posits that the less committed and the less definite you are, the more options you'll have available. In fact, in the decades following World War II, our parents raised many of us to believe we could do or be anything, with no limits. However, the opposite turns out to be true. Vagueness doesn't open doors or keep them open. It breeds confusion. It invites misunderstanding. When you think you're "keeping your options open," in fact you're waffling.

Over time, you might have noticed the results. Things grew more and more fuzzy

- in your interpersonal relationships, including those in the business world (Does she like me or not? If he won't be clear, how can I trust him?);

- in communications with others (Just what's he mean by *that?*) and miscommunications (Why can't people see what I *really* mean?);

- in your work (Should I promise this customer that I'll deliver, even though I'm not sure?);

- in your mission in life (If I keep my options open in lots of areas, won't that let me "have it all"?).

Clarity, however, both opens the doors you want to go through and closes the ones you don't want to go through. In the end, what's operating is the same principle that makes a hydroelectric dam work: Fling all the gates wide and the water's potential force is dispersed, but focus the water by funneling it through a well-defined channel and you generate power.

Once you experience the moment of recognition and see that this is how NO operates in you, the light goes on. You can practice NO because it's something you were born with. You become conscious of its power. You internalize your understanding. Most importantly, you can apply it to an infinite number of personal, business and career situations.

Eventually, NO becomes a NO-brainer, second nature except in the sense that now you're *aware* of what you're doing: making clear, conscious choices defined not only by what you want but also by what you *don't* want. In the process, your ability to choose effectively impacts virtually every aspect of your life:

- Career choice

- Work issues

- Family

- Relationships

- Creativity

- Money management

- Time management

We make no claims, but it might even influence your health in the long run, since the Power of NO is, by definition, a stress-buster. Think, for instance, of the last time you hung your head and mumbled, "I truly wish I had said NO." It gets you to prioritize quickly, almost instantaneously. You make clear, precise choices in line with your most desired outcomes and values. Your energy isn't diverted into worrying and stressing out over which choice is "right" – you already know that. The decision is swift and satisfying. And because it's already attuned to your core values, there's no stressful sense of contradiction.

The operative words are "clear," "choice" and "values." Put them together, and the essence of NO reads something like this: **the power to make clear choices that are aligned to personal values and goals.** NO brings clarity to your life and empowers you to choose wisely, in line with your core values.

NO-TOLOGY IN BODY, MIND AND SPIRIT

Artists call it "negative space." In sculpture, for instance, the areas in between solid forms themselves play a role in the total composition. Similarly, architects are very conscious of the fact that walls, floors and ceilings simply define the space in which we live and work.

In music, it's the pause between the notes. In philosophy, it's the flip side of a premise that is always, by definition, present. Many, if not most, world philosophies acknowledge NO: Buddhist teachings point out the inherently dualistic nature of this world we live in; Taoism discusses the fundamental universal principles of yin and yang.

In engineering, a bridge is designed to *not* collapse under the stresses of a specific site and a building is constructed to withstand major earthquakes. Even the human body understands NO. The mission of leukocytes, for instance, is to eliminate the microbes and organisms that *don't* belong in your bloodstream.

In fact, our world rings with the ontological significance of NO – with NO-tology.

When you don't pay attention to the flip side of the equation, things fall apart. The artistic composition doesn't "work." The bridge collapses. The white blood cells malfunction to the point where either there are too few to ward off invaders or so many that they start to attack good cells.

The same thing occurs with you. When you fail to take into account the other half, then this complex manifestation of thinking, feeling, doing and becoming – a human being – gets fuzzy around the edges. You spend your life befuddled, pulled in umpteen directions by the myriad forces, influences, people and events coming at you every day. When you get a spare moment to regroup, you might decide you need to assert yourself, to be more proactive. Maybe you visualize how you'd like your life to go. You might even get determined and take action. And all the while you focus on only positive outcomes.

There's a problem with this kind of "positive thinking" approach, though. It's incomplete. It doesn't take into account the other half of the equation. It doesn't take into account what you *don't* want.

Consider how difficult it actually is to define yourself in only positive ways. Try answering the perennial question "Who am I?" in terms of only who you are already: dark hair, dark eyes, enjoy spicy food, manager at Big Company, etc. Implicit in every one of these is what you're *not* mentioning: other hair/eye colors, the variety of cuisines around the world, the fact that you're not an entrepreneur, not employed in the nonprofit realm, and so on.

In fact, it's probably impossible to focus only on who you are without any reference to who you're not. Even to call yourself a human being is to state, by default, that you're not vegetable, mineral or one of the other species defined as animal.

NO is integral to who you are. YES and NO together make a whole. YES is the marble that is hewn to form a sculpture; NO is the act of carving away all the marble that does not belong. YES is a house made up of spaces called rooms; NO is the ceiling, walls and floors that define the rooms.

On a practical level, NO creates limits. Instead of YESing everything to the point where you're lost in all the possibilities of what could be, you pare down possibility into a manageable package. Where YES accommodates and embraces, NO gives you something to push up against. And without clear limits, without well-defined parameters that *you* choose and *you* enforce, fuzziness sets in again.

You can't create something – a thriving business, a book, a self – without defining exactly what it is *and* what it is not. With clear limits, however, you've got something. You've got a house to live in. You've got a sense of self. You've got values. This is the essence of Limit Theory™: **The clearer you are about what you want and don't want, YES and NO, yellow bull's-eye and red ring, the more successful you'll be in whatever project you have in mind.**

NO NONSENSE

It's possible, of course, to overdo it. Where an overly positive thinker indulges in too much YES (leading to a **Big Fuzzy Target** – see inside front cover), the NO fanatic limits choices so severely that there are very few left (creating an **Anal Target**). You can swing to the opposite extreme of positivity and end up NO-ing life to death.

What can happen when you overdo YES?

- You become overly cooperative and accommodating to the point of having few or no opinions of your own.

- You're very nice but also vague and unclear, which leads to being misunderstood.

- Lacking definition and discrimination, you turn wishy-washy and soon find you can't accomplish your goals.

- Your target, the **Big Fuzzy Target**, visually depicts a loss of discipline and focus, favoring inspiration over discipline.

And what can happen with too much NO?

- You do everything "by the book," so much so that your life is over-regulated, over-ruled and unimaginative.

- You adhere to an old set of values and resist change – even though the one guarantee in life is that things *will* change, whether you like it or not.

- Managing on the job becomes a series of commands – "do this" as opposed to a more collaborative "let's accomplish this."

- Your target, the **Anal Target**, squelches inspiration and original thinking. It favors discipline over inspiration.

The point is that your NOes and your YESes require equal attention. The two need to be in balance. Where YES inspires you and opens you to seemingly infinite possibility, NO focuses, clarifies and defines the possibilities. NO provides the discipline required if you're going to make a beautiful vision a reality.

The ideal, then, is a balance between both YES and NO – a kind of *disciplined inspiration.*

This sounds great until you start to put it into practice, because that's when your lifelong training in YES begins to rear up. The NO model no longer seems elegantly rational. Instead, it seems threatening to all those nice, pleasant YES ways you learned in younger years. At a visceral level, you might find yourself objecting that NO isn't such a great idea after all.

You might even find yourself descending into NO nonsense – the myths, misrepresentations and misinterpretations that can undermine the Power of NO and hold you captive in the powerless state of the **Big Fuzzy Target**. For instance:

Myth 1: Saying NO is impolite. But if politeness means displaying respect for someone else, then clarity demonstrates far more respect than mindless agreement. How? When you're clear about how you disagree with someone's opinion, you're implicitly showing respect for his or her intelligence. You also open the door to *creative* disagreement, the kind where two well-defined opinions can meet, dispute and eventually locate something neither one would have discovered on its own.

Myth 2: NO implies criticism. As you undo the mental patterns and associations we have with the word NO, however, you begin to recognize that it's simply the flip side of YES, as in north and south poles, heads and tails, positive and negative space. None of those are value judgments, nor is NO a value judgment directed at another person. It simply reflects a decision you've made based on the criteria you hold most important in your life. The other choice would be to compromise your values in order to avoid appearing critical. Would you want that?

Myth 3: People won't like you if you tell them NO. Even folk wisdom contradicts this myth. Who hasn't noticed how people appreciate men who say NO and stick to their convictions? How we secretly admire women who make their own choices, refusing to conform mindlessly to others' value systems? They're often called people of integrity. And anyway, others certainly won't like you if, in the interest of being "nice," you end up misleading them by saying YES when you'd rather say NO. They'll like you and respect you a whole lot more if you're honest with them.

Myth 4: Women who say NO are bitchy. See above. And see also the way most people over time will qualify their initial condemnation of NO-saying women. "She thinks for herself," they finally say. Or: "I might not agree with her, but I like her strength." Habitual YES-women, on the other hand, seem doomed to being written off as "nice" but not memorable, or "pleasant and accommodating" but not management material. Finally, to say NO doesn't mean you have to be belligerent about it. Some of the best nay-sayers know how to do so while also projecting genuine warmth.

Myth 5: NO loses customers. See the following chapters!

Myth 6: NO eliminates your wiggle room. The real question here is, why is that a problem? Saying NO means defining your limits and sticking to them. It means committing, then staying the course in work and life, rather than reacting to whatever life brings next. It means being *proactive*, thinking clearly, saying NO to what doesn't fit in with your picture and standing by that choice in order to achieve the desired outcome. As a result, most nay-sayers are high-achievers. So yes, NO does eliminate wiggle room. But is that really such a bad thing?

Myth 7: NO is "negative," which is something "positive thinkers" try diligently to avoid. Because NO is all about rejecting what doesn't belong in your picture, it tends to root out things that lurk beneath the surface, issues that no one wants to face. It uncovers potential problems that many positive thinkers deny – until those problems simply *have* to be addressed. By then, of course, it's often too late. So NO does reveal the shadow side of situations. This might not be pleasant, but in the end it helps head off problems before they do much damage.

Interestingly, most of these myths, these objections to NO, concern the individual in social situations. At home alone, on the other hand, we're usually a lot clearer about what we *don't* want in our worlds. If you can't stand the color red, you're not going paint your living room walls that color. If your ambition is to become a world-class oceanographer, you presumably have eliminated inland, mountainous regions from your list of possible places to live.

The point is that bigger problems surface – along with the need for NO – when there's more to your life than just yourself, when multiple forces come at you from your environment, insisting that you pay attention to all of them. This is where Limit Theory™ shines, giving you the tools to clarify, choose and stand by your choice.

THE NO ZONE

Among the most prominent forces competing for your attention are family, friends and relationships in general, along with the organization(s) in which you function. When we enter a group setting, the external and internal pressures multiply exponentially. Overt demands come at us from the boss, subtle cues emanate from the guy in the office next door, interpersonal insinuations slide from the corporate grapevine straight into our consciousness. And what once appeared to be a whole, discrete self – you – is pulled this way and that from moment to moment.

Often these multiple social factors throw so much at you that you might fall back on classic reactive patterns: You either habitually accommodate, YESing everyone, or you become a habitual nay-sayer. Neither strategy is strategic: They do not involve choice, only knee-jerk reactivity. And the more you rely on reactivity to pull you through life, the more it spirals out of your control.

But something happens when you practice NO within yourself, when you proactively make more and more private choices that affect you alone. As you remember the fundamental place of NO in the way things are and the way we're made – the Tao of NO, if you will – you also increase your ability to clarify, choose and stand by your choice in relation to other individuals, then groups and even entire organizations. It becomes possible to recognize not only your own limits but others', too. Respect is the end result, even compassion.

How do you get to this point?

CLARITY, CHOICE, COMMITMENT –
The path to the Ideal Target

CLARITY Whether it's for you the person-father-husband-teacher or you the organizational leader-CEO-manager, the **Ideal Target** you construct will need crystal-clear limits between what's acceptable and what is not. These limits may be either quantifiable (I won't spend more than a certain amount of money on personal entertainment) or qualifiable (the people I surround myself with must be supporting and educational). You must be able to quickly and easily tell the difference between what falls within your bull's-eye and what does not. If your cutoff for entertainment funds is $100 a month, then $100.10 is a NO. People in your social sphere with agendas that undermine your goals are a NO.

In the archery target metaphor we use in this book, the concept of clarity is symbolized by the crystal-clear limit between the yellow bull's-eye and the red ring surrounding it. Fuzziness is the antithesis of clarity. Fuzzy limits cause stress, misunderstanding and miscommunication, not to mention the fact that neither you nor the archery judge can ever identify a bull's-eye.

CHOICE Once you've clarified these limits by establishing clear YES/NO signposts, where to set those limits becomes the issue. Choosing the figure of $100 a month as your entertainment cutoff must be based on your data, your standards, your needs and desires.

Where clarity defined what falls inside (and outside) of your target, choice sets the size of the bull's eye. Is your entertainment budget $1,000 a month, or $10 or $100? What diameter is the red ring of NO that surrounds and defines the yellow bull's-eye of YES? What do you include? What do you exclude? Is it one inch in diameter, thereby possibly qualifying as an **Anal**? Is it almost the entire diameter of the whole target and so perhaps a little too **Anything Goes**? Or is it approaching **Ideal**?

That is totally your choice, and choice is what endows you as a human being with the blessing of free will.

COMMITMENT You've set the size of your bull's-eye (choice), and you've established very clear limits between YES and NO, between yellow bull's-eye and red ring surrounding it. Now comes the tough part. clarity and choice are admirable elements of living a successful existence or managing a productive organization. But without a third element, commitment, they are of little value. Without commitment, clarifying (sharpening the limits between yes and no, between yellow bull's-eye and red ring) and choosing the scope of your limits (the size of your bull's-eye) are exercises in idle speculation. In developing your plans to make use of the Power of NO, *not committing* has got to be a NO. It's outside your bull's-eye. It's in the red ring. It's unacceptable.

When your entertainment spending limit is set at $100 and so far this month you've spent $50, spending another $35 on dinner is easy to justify. Declining an offer to go to a football game which would cost you another $85 is fairly easy too; the degree to which this violates your limit is quite clear. But spending $51 on concert tickets is another matter. commitment takes courage. Stick-to-it-ive-ness. Guts. It's easy to see the things that do not approach your limits, or greatly exceed them, and rule them a YES or a NO. But a YES/NO decision right near the limit is a test of your courage. Your commitment either stands or falls. There is no middle ground. And with your **Ideal Target**, you don't allow any fuzziness.

Just as clarity and choice are useless without commitment, so are any two of these elements without the third. Probably the most dangerous possibility is choice and commitment without clarity. This would mean committing your resources, perhaps time, money and/or emotional energy, to some exercise without having a crystal-clear limit between YES and NO. It's unfocused and rudderless. It can lead to miscommunication, frustration and, of course, failure.

Yet the combination of clarity and commitment without choice is fairly common in many pop-psychology self-improvement manuals. The past two decades of "creative visualization" training we've undergone, attempting to focus on what we are and what we will be, have left us lacking this one important element. Adding choice to the mix defines the size of the bull's-eye and sets limits so that you can also be aware of what you are not and won't be. Without those limits defined, you're likely to waste resources on projects, relationships, investments that take you away from your bull's-eye.

In this book you'll learn to *not* waste your time, energy and personal resources anymore. You'll learn about the Positive Power of NO and Limit Theory™, and how to infuse these philosophies into your everyday life. You'll read case studies of organizations that knew how to say NO and ones that did not.

At the end, you'll toss this book on the pile of business knowledge books you've been investing in for years, and go out and buy another. Or you'll pick it up and read through it again. Frankly, it barely scratches the surface of the benefits of knowing why, when, where and how to say NO.

But then, you already know them. They're in you.

*   *   *   *   *   *   *

i   Know thyself (Gnothi seauton) – Delphic Oracle, inscription on the Oracle of Apollo at Delphi, Greece, 6th century B.C.

ABOUT SARAH BASSETT

Sarah Bassett is currently communications director for Red Cross in St. Louis, Missouri. She has held positions in the entertainment industry as publicist, communications guru and general advisor to production companies. As editor, writer and creative director, she has developed numerous publications, from corporate and consumer magazines to marketing collaterals. She has counseled startups, nonprofits and small to medium-sized businesses in communications and marketing strategies.

Sarah has studied Buddhism, eastern philosophies and many meditation disciplines, all of which she uses to help clients focus and make right choices.

Her expertise with Power of NO is as an executive coach, dealing more with matters of personal productivity than with matters of corporate productivity.

CHAPTER III.

The Art of Strategy: The Formula Revealed

Art Kimbrough

S trategy is all around us. We use the term all the time. We have strategies for this and strategies for that. We have strategies for growth and strategies for recovery. We have offensive strategies, defensive strategies, marketing strategies, e-commerce strategies, operational strategies, competitive strategies, etc. The list of strategies is virtually endless.

But in spite of strategy's pervasive use, many people have ignored a remarkably simple formula for effective strategy. The result has often been loss of focus, dilution of resources, weakened market position, erosion of profits and, in severe cases, total business failure.

This formula is so powerful, so effective and so profound that its simplicity makes us blind to its significance. Few people seem to understand how to use it, how to interpret it and how to apply its principles in a meaningful, sustainable way.

I. THE FORMULA

What is this formula and why is it so powerful?

Very simply, it is the *Positive* Power of NO!

Effective strategy is as much about creating a framework for deciding what NOT to do as it is about deciding what to do. The Positive Power of NO is derived from the limits it sets. Its strength comes from the clarity it provides in setting direction and eliminating distractions. It puts corners around ideas and makes them real.

NO is the boundary of yes. Just think of a target's bull's-eye. If the yellow bull's-eye represents yes, and the red circle immediately surrounding it represents NO, then the boundary between the yellow bull's-eye and the red circle is the outer limit of yes and the beginning of NO.

Strategy and strategic planning are about making tough choices. Which products or services should I provide and which ones should I NOT provide? Which markets should I serve and which ones should I NOT serve? Which customers within my market should I seek, and which ones should I NOT seek? Where should I locate and where should I NOT locate? Whom should I hire and whom should I NOT hire?

Strategy also means deciding how much of the value chain I occupy and how much I do NOT occupy. It means selecting which pricing plan to use and which pricing plan to NOT use. It means deciding how to invest my capital and how NOT to invest my capital.

The things you choose NOT to do are just as important as the things you choose TO DO. The sum total of all the choices you make establish your identity. They make you unique and give you a distinctive strategic position relative to the competition. Strategy, quite simply, is what makes you different.

When organizations lose their ability to say NO, they become unfocused and fragmented. With unrelenting pressure on executives and managers to grow revenue and profits, it becomes easy to jump on every opportunity, lower standards or take any kind of business. Unfortunately, trying to be everything to everyone usually means being nothing to no one!

Harvard professor Michael Porter, one of the leading gurus of strategy, says, "The essence of strategy is that you must set limits on what you're trying to accomplish. The company without a strategy is willing to try anything." [i]

A company that will try anything is a company headed for serious trouble. Innovation, experimentation and research are vital elements of successful organizations. But when it comes to strategy, a lack of limits can prove fatal. A crystal-clear focus is the path to enormous rewards.

II. THE FORMULA AT WORK

All companies, whether large, small or start-up, face consequences depending on whether they have clear strategic boundaries. These consequences can be either positive or negative, but there are always consequences. The choices made and limits set can dramatically affect the trajectory of their future.

The lesson to be learned is simple: **How you make choices and set limits will determine how much "Positive" you generate from the Power of NO.**

Let's take a closer look at how the strategic use of "NO" shaped the direction and success of several companies. With only one exception (Lan & Spar), the case studies and examples that follow are the result of my firsthand observation and research.

"NO" AT WORK IN LARGE COMPANIES

Large companies face different challenges than small companies. They have large amounts of resources to throw at opportunities and problems, but their very size slows them down. Because of the distribution and dilution of authority, they are always at risk of an expanding internal bureaucracy. Staying nimble is a constant battle for large, prosperous companies.

As pressure mounts in rapidly growing companies to sustain growth rates, NO has a tendency to give way to YES at any cost! Staying focused and aimed in the right direction takes courage. It takes the courage to say NO!

The Positive Consequence of Saying NO: Edward Jones

Becoming customer-focused doesn't mean giving all customers everything they think they want. What it does mean is providing *exceptional value* in a *specific way* to a *defined group* of customers.

A great example of this is Edward Jones, the St. Louis based investment and securities firm (www.edwardjones.com). With over $2 billion in revenue and more than 8,400 brokers in individual offices throughout the United States, Canada and the United Kingdom, Edward Jones is the last true partnership on Wall Street. It is also one of the most consistently profitable firms in the volatile securities industry. Michael Porter, in a Harvard case study, raves that Edward Jones is one of the most strategically solid and robust companies in America.[ii] It is a role model in the design and execution of strategy.

What makes Edward Jones unique, and how does the Power of NO enter into its strategy? The answer is simple. The firm has an explicit, clear strategy that differentiates it from the competition and keeps employees focused on the single objective of serving the individual investor.

Peter Drucker describes Edward Jones as "a federation of highly autonomous entrepreneurial units bound together by a strong set of values and beliefs."[iii] Those beliefs include a clear articulation of what they will and WON'T do.

First, Edward Jones serves only individual investors, NOT institutional investors. Second, every office is a one-broker office that operates as a stand-alone profit center – there are NO big boiler-room sales operations. Third, Edward Jones DOES NOT manufacture the products it sells; instead it acts as a distributor for the products of a few select firms such as Putnam and Morgan Stanley. Fourth, Edward Jones sells only long-term, large-cap equities and highly rated bonds that fit a buy-and-hold investment strategy; it does not promote risky IPOs, commodity futures or options. And finally, Edward Jones remains a partnership so employees and executives will think and act like owners. They chose NOT to be a publicly traded company subject to the short-term demands of outside stockholders.

During the Internet craze of the late 1990s, there was a lot of pressure on Edward Jones to offer online trading. Even after the company decided that this did not fit its strategy, internal advocates of online trading put pressure on management to go ahead and develop the technology. It would be a backup plan, they said, in case competition forced Edward Jones to move in that direction. After an extended and often contentious debate at an off-site strategic planning session, the company's executive committee decided to close that door completely by not investing in a back-up plan. Online trading would not be an option, now or in the future. The wisdom of their choice became crystal-clear as the dot-com meltdown proved that online trading for most investors was more of a fad than a deep trend.

Edward Jones made explicit choices about what it would do and what it would NOT do. It made conscious trade-offs that have resulted in a defendable, differentiated strategy. It has been true to the strategy for more than 20 years and has no intention of changing anytime soon. John Bachmann, managing partner and chief architect of the strategy, was quoted as saying, "These principles are cast in stone. We don't debate these things." [iv]

A quote from Michael Porter summarizes the lesson of Edward Jones: "Strategy is about the basic value you're trying to deliver to customers, and about which customers you're trying to serve. That positioning, at that level, is where continuity needs to be strongest. Otherwise, it's hard for your organization to grasp what the strategy is. And it's hard for customers to know what you stand for." [v]

Having clear boundaries and knowing why, when, where and how to say NO keeps you focused on your core strategy and mission. It gives you identity, establishes your brand, provides a framework for making consistent decisions, and tells your customers, employees, suppliers and stockholders what you stand for.

Think back over your own experience and see if you can identify other companies or organizations that had limits as clearly defined as those at Edward Jones. Were they as successful in carrying out their strategy? Would you want to invest in them if you could? What were their limits? What did they decide NOT to do? How did they communicate it? What was the result?

The Negative Consequence of Not Saying NO: Control Data Corp.

Control Data Corporation was once a prominent computer technology company. At its peak in the 1960s through mid-1980s, it was a Fortune 100 company with more than $3 billion in revenue, $6 billion in assets and 60,000 employees worldwide. Started in 1957 with pioneering supercomputer technology, Control Data had evolved into the dominant force in mass storage devices for mainframe computers by the early 1970s.

By the late '70s, however, Control Data had expanded into a vast array of businesses, many of which were only remotely connected to the company's core strengths. Managers were given, or took, the latitude to apply computer technology to every conceivable human, societal, governmental or business condition. The result, instead of breadth and strength, was a diversification so broad and unfocused that the dilution of financial resources made it nearly impossible to respond to competitive attacks on the core business.

In the mid '80s, when the Japanese came out with superior mass storage technology at substantially lower prices, Control Data was spread so thin it could not react quickly. Ultimately, nearly every company asset was sold, closed or liquidated, and the once-proud company ceased to exist in any substantive way. By trying to become everything to everyone, Control Data became nothing to no one.

Think back over your own experience and see if you can identify other companies or organizations that faced difficulty because they lost focus. When did it happen? Why did it happen? What was the ultimate consequence? Did they get back on track? How did they regain their focus? What did they decide NOT to do? How did they communicate it?

Staying the Course: World Wide Technology

The June 2001 cover of Black Enterprise magazine describes David Steward, CEO of World Wide Technology (www.WWT.com), as "The 800 Million Dollar Man." This was in recognition of his accomplishment in creating the largest black-owned enterprise in America. What is even more significant about this story is that he did it in less than 10 years, starting from scratch with limited resources. In the course of one decade, Steward went from struggling entrepreneur to business superstar and role model for hundreds of thousands of people who aspire to the American dream.

"Things were so lean in the beginning that my car was literally repossessed right in front of my eyes. As I looked out of my office window in surprise, my employees and I watched helplessly as they attached my car to the tow truck and drove off. I was unable to stop them long enough to even get my briefcase out of the car," says Steward.[vi]

Anxious, but undaunted, Steward hitched a ride with one of his employees to the tow lot so they could retrieve the briefcase. There was no money to get the car back, but the briefcase had vital information that the company needed.

What makes this story unusual isn't that his car was repossessed, but rather the reason it was repossessed. Steward faced tough choices in the months preceding that event. Some events had occurred that bled the company of its cash and put World Wide Technology at risk. He had to make a choice between making payroll and making his personal car payments. Because of his belief in his employees and his belief in the company, he put them ahead of his personal needs. For months, Steward and his family shared one car as World Wide Technology fought to survive and grow.

By staying the course, choosing NOT to put self above company, and eliminating distractions that might take the company off course, Steward and World Wide Technology grew at an accelerated pace and became a role model company for others to emulate.

I've had the privilege of knowing David Steward as both a strategic business partner and a personal friend. What I have observed is a man who has absolute clarity in his strategic vision and a deep foundation of beliefs and values that set clear boundaries for the choices he, his family and his employees make. In his case, religious faith is the anchor that puts every choice into clear perspective. Because he has clear beliefs, gaining the necessary commitment to carry out the choices he and his employees make becomes a great deal easier.

His commitments are then aligned with the core targets he has established in his business and personal life. At World Wide Technology, the line between the yellow bull's-eye of YES and the red circle of NO is absolutely crystal clear.

In your own experience, can you identify other companies or organizations that have values that come to life and manifest themselves in the behavior of everyone? What did they do differently or better? Would you want to work there if you could? How would you apply those principles in your business?

"NO" AT WORK IN SMALL COMPANIES

Small and medium-sized enterprises (SMEs) face many of the same challenges as large companies, but the issues and implications of their decisions are greatly amplified. There are no deep pockets to cover big mistakes. Resources are limited and time is scarce. Small missteps can have huge consequences. Time is often the scarcest resource.

In March 2000, the National Research Council (NRC), under the auspices of the National Institute of Standards and Technology (NIST, www.nist.gov), published the results of a three-year examination of the issues facing SMEs.[vii] Their findings about strategic planning are particularly enlightening.

The NRC found that most SMEs do little formal business planning. A 1999 survey of 500 businesses with fewer than 500 employees revealed that only 13% had an annual budget in writing, only 14% had a business plan in writing, and only 12% had a long-range plan in writing. Many respondents indicated that their annual plan is in the CEO's head and that the annual budget consists essentially of "sell as much as possible, make payroll, and keep the lights on." (Wall Street Journal, Sept. 7, 1999)

While these results will not surprise consultants and other professionals who work with SMEs, the scope and depth of the strategy problem is far worse than most business owners would like to acknowledge. In today's business environment, a lack of planning and a corresponding lack of focus can prove deadly.

Because of the rapid rate of change in many industries, opportunities arise and disappear frequently. But taking advantage of these opportunities can be expensive. Opportunities must be carefully selected so as not to exhaust a SME's limited resources. Identifying the requirements for competing and determining capability to compete are vital steps in saying NO to certain opportunities and narrowing the choices to the single best path.

Developing a strategy or business plan need not be an elaborate process, but it should involve more than just an annual budget. At a minimum, the plan should define the company's products, markets, geography, competitive position and strategic focus. This information allows for the creation of a vision for the company, and selection of specific steps and timetables for achieving the vision. The company's strategy should zero in on core competencies, leverage those strengths, and identify ways to measure progress.

For SMEs, the plan must focus on a small number of activities. The optimum strategy for a small SME may be to excel in one carefully defined capability and retain merely adequate capabilities in other areas.

In simple terms, small and medium-sized enterprises must learn why, when, where and how to say NO. They must pick their strategic target carefully and stay true to their course.

Lessons Learned: Wainwright Industries

Wainwright Industries Inc. is a small manufacturing company in St. Peters, Missouri. In 1994, Wainwright Industries (www.wainwright industries.com) won the Malcolm Baldrige National Quality Award, which is the business equivalent of an Oscar. Wainwright's sustained level of quality and performance made it a company that was studied and benchmarked by thousands of other companies around the world.

What set Wainwright Industries apart was its clarity of focus and the methods it developed for measuring performance. These measurement systems played a key role in building a culture of trust and employee involvement that was based on open and honest communication.

With more than 10,000 implemented improvements per year from an employee population of only 300, Wainwright clearly was doing something right. Its CIP (Continuous Improvement Process) program was unique because it allowed employees to actually make and implement improvements before seeking approval from a boss. That's a big improvement on the traditional suggestion box, where ideas tend to be ignored and forgotten.

At this point you may be thinking, "That sounds more like an example of the *Positive Power of YES* than the *Positive Power of NO*." Nothing could be further from the truth.

At Wainwright Industries, employees' freedom to innovate and create was only possible because there was a robust system in place that established clear limits within which employees could act with total autonomy. In other words, a powerful feeling of YES was created because there was a clearly established and communicated framework of NO in place.

How did this system work?

First and foremost, it was based on the premise that employees want to do a good job and want to be trusted to use their own intelligence and skill to do that job. Bosses aren't the only people who want control over their work environment.

Second, Wainwright developed easy-to-remember principles and easy-to-follow procedures. The focus was on all the small improvements that are usually overlooked. "Don't try to re-engineer the design of the plant, just move the hazard out of the way!" Employees had to make improvements within their own individual work area. If you saw an improvement that was outside your area, you had to collaborate with the person in that area to make the improvement. Employees had no budget to spend to make these improvements, but they had complete freedom to use existing resources to make things better. If they needed any money to make the improvement work, they could turn to their supervisor for assistance. Each supervisor had a $1,000 annual budget that could be used any way they saw fit to help employees implement improvement projects.

Finally, employees were heavily trained and creatively rewarded for making many small improvements. Employees knew exactly what they could and could not do. With clear limits, Wainwright employees can use their creativity to make a world-class difference!

By using systems that set clearly understood limits, and by fostering a system of communication based on trust rather than "gotcha," Wainwright Industries created a "People First, Profits Follow Naturally" culture that enriched the lives and fortunes of employees, customers, suppliers and stockholders.

In your own experience, can you think of other companies or organizations that have implemented systems that made a big difference in their ability to gain broad levels of employee involvement? What did they do? How did they work? Were there clear lines between YES and NO? How would you apply those principles in your business?

Develop a Team, NOT a Successor: Quantum Technologies, Inc.

Jack Sieber, founder of Quantum Technologies, Inc., a St. Louis office printing solutions provider, was preparing the company for his eventual retirement. For years he groomed a successor that would run the business like he ran it. To Sieber's surprise, his chosen successor announced he was leaving. This threw a big wrench in his plans.

After much thought, Sieber decided NOT to seek a new successor. Instead, he pulled together his best players, formed a leadership team, and took them through a formal strategic planning and team-building process.

The next six months profoundly changed the company and Sieber's view of leadership. His team stepped up to the plate and took responsibility in ways he could not imagine. People grew right before his eyes. The company found new opportunities for competitive advantage, and business became FUN again. By saying NO to finding a successor, and instead creating an environment where his team uses their talents to make a difference, Jack now has six successors, not just one!

Are you limiting your potential by setting a target so small that you put the entire strategy at risk? How do you know if your target is too small or too large? Does your target strategy rely on many or few? Is it clear enough for everyone to see?

Great Intentions, but ...: Patriot Machine

In the late '80s and early '90s the "Quality" movement gave give way to the "Customer Focus" movement. Companies all over America began to raise the level of service they offered. As inspiration, they used legendary examples such as Nordstrom, Stew Leonard's Dairy, Disney and Southwest Airlines, along with supportive data from PIMS (Profit Impact of Market Strategy) and TARP (Technical Assistance Research Project) on the profitability of being customer-focused.

"Customer Focus" was the single most pervasive management fad of the decade prior to the Internet explosion. For many companies, especially those that understood the strategic context within which they positioned their customer- focused initiatives; this shift in thinking had a profoundly positive effect. For others, the effect was not as positive.

A case in point is Patriot Machine, Inc., a company that manufactures complex, custom-designed metal parts for the aircraft industry. The leaders, managers and employees of this company take great pride in the reputation they built for doing whatever it takes to satisfy the customer. Their quality ratings are at the top of the class. They won bids because they would do what their competitors would not. On the surface, they were a case study in how to satisfy the customer.

During their strategic planning session, it became clear they were giving away the store to satisfy unreasonable demands from customers who valued their work but weren't willing to pay for that value. When it became clear how their bidding process was killing the bottom line, the leaders of this company decided it was time to start telling certain customers NO. Bob Burns, Patriot's co-founder and chief engineer, grasped the implications of this decision so quickly that he left the meeting to retrieve a bid that was going out the door that day. Over lunch he called the customer, had a frank discussion about price, service, and quality, and told the customer that the bid specifications had to change or a higher price would be required. The customer chose to pay the higher price because he valued the service and the relationship. By learning to say NO to unprofitable business, Patriot Machine immediately improved its profitability and became stronger.

Are there examples like this in your company? Are there clearly defined limits between good business and bad business? How do you know? How can you find out if you don't know? Would knowing this information help you become a better company?

Too Many Customers: Lan & Spar

Constantinos Markides, chairman of the Strategic and International Management Department at the London School of Business, in his insightful book *All The Right Moves*, tells how a small Danish bank, Lan & Spar, made a clear and explicit choice about which customers it would serve and which customers it would NOT serve.[viii]

In 1989, Lan and Spar contacted all of its corporate clients (who represented 25% of its deposits) and asked them to leave the bank and open new accounts with its competitors. Instead of serving both corporations and consumers, Lan & Spar consciously decided to focus its strategy only on white-collar consumers. By 1991, Lan & Spar was the most profitable bank in Denmark. Today, it remains one of the most profitable banks in the country, and its market share within its target customer base has grown fourfold. By deciding whom NOT to serve,

Lan & Spar created a clear identity and focus that propelled its growth and kept it from having to fight expensive competitive battles with large multinational financial institutions that wanted to own the corporate banking market.

Is your company serving the right customer segments? Are you serving too many low- profit customers? Do you know which customers are your most profitable customers? If you don't know, how could you find out?

"NO" AT WORK IN START-UPS

Surviving "Dot-bust": ICLogistics

For the past three years I have been heavily involved with the creation and launch of ICLogistics, an Internet B2B software company (www.ICLogistics.com). My partner John Clendenin, a former professor at Harvard's Graduate School of Business, and I have met with and pitched investors of all types, from sophisticated venture capitalists and investment bankers to "friends, family and fools" who knew nothing about investing in start-ups.

When John, our other partners, and I began our odyssey in late 1998, professional investors and amateurs alike were clamoring to get on the Internet bandwagon. Until the dot-bust of 2000, they were throwing money at almost anything, including college students with ideas written on the back of paper napkins. Now, after a severe correction in the financial markets, investors are as reluctant today to throw money at deals as they were eager to grab a piece of the action before.

Venture capitalist Tom Siegel, whom I came to know quite well, calls the pre-bust investment philosophy the "greater fools theory of investing." [ix] Every round of investment pre-supposed that another round would follow and that the next "greater fool" would buy out the early investor. Since the meltdown, the investment environment has become more of a "greatest fear" theory, i.e. "If I invest anything I fear I will lose it!"

At ICLogistics, we started the "money hunt" just before the investment climate entered the deep freeze. While we thought we had a compelling plan and a great management team, we did not have a completed or tested product, nor did we have any customers. The "easy venture money" dried up while we were still at too early a stage, and conservative money just wasn't willing to take any risk. To survive, we had to bootstrap our way forward and build our company the old-fashioned way.

We now faced new obstacles. Without capital, our rate of development was slowed to a crawl. We began to feel pressure to change our focus and widen the target to include consulting work unrelated to our core products. We also felt a lot of pressure from the venture community to dramatically lower the valuation of the company (reduce the asking price for each share of stock). This would mean giving up control of the company for a relatively small amount of investment cash.

After a month or so of debate and struggle, we made a decision. We would NOT dilute the focus of our CEO and top technology talent by selling their services to work on unrelated consulting assignments, and we would NOT lower the valuation rate or give up control of the company. We would stay the course and keep developing the product, even if it would take a year or more longer than planned. Spending was trimmed even further, what few salaries existed would be virtually eliminated and converted to stock, and software development would be taken offshore.

The result is a company that survived "dot-bust," and now has a working prototype, a few strategically important customers and enough angel capital to keep afloat. It also has a group of specialized venture capital firms making commitments to invest significant funds to fuel growth.

By making a set of decisions about what we would NOT do, we moved closer toward our goal rather than further away.

Before the so-called "market correction" of 2000, professional investors demanded a clear and *compelling business plan* with a *focused strategy* that *grew rapidly* within a *well-defined target market*. Since the summer of

2000, *speed of growth* has been replaced by a clear path to *profitability* as one of the most important metrics.

The lesson is this: Your company must have a strategic plan that articulates what it will do and what it will NOT do. Companies that wander into the "will NOT do" area without a powerful reason for shifting strategic direction will be punished severely by their investors. Even in a start-up, what you choose NOT to do is as important as what you choose to do.

Have you known of start-up companies that failed because they had no limits? Did you get caught up in the "hype" and assume every "dot-something" was going to be a success? What lessons did you learn that you could apply in your business?

Finding the Right Partners: Rising Media.net

Ken Lauher, founder and CEO of Rising Media (www.risingmedia.net), launched his company in early 2001 with the idea of becoming the dominant online and off-line catalyst for networking events and business connections in second-tier markets.

To make this happen, Ken knew he needed to form strategic alliances with companies that could give his company credibility and access to the market. Because Rising Media is a media company, many people and organizations sought him out to try and piggyback on his firm's ability to generate publicity inexpensively.

It wasn't long before Ken realized that he had to set clear standards for selecting strategic partners. The first thing he did was to decide who would NOT be eligible. He drew up criteria about quality, capability, contribution, reputation and character that would serve as a filter to exclude 90% of the firms seeking to attach themselves to his company.

The result for Rising Media is a brand that has premium alliances with top-quality firms. To provide knowledge content for customers in his target audience, he chose to partner with an emerging seminar company whose leadership team was well known in the technology market, and whose business goals aligned with Rising Media's. Subsequently, top firms in other areas were selected, and a virtual team of high-powered alliances was in place.

Rising Media has quickly become "the place" for many to go for online, local business information in its initial market. It also is "the place" to be seen once each month at Rising Media's unique networking events.

What criteria do you use to determine whom you will partner with and whom you will NOT partner with? Are your strategic partnerships providing real value, or are they taking away from your focus and identity?

III. PUTTING THE FORMULA TO WORK IN YOUR COMPANY

FIRST STEPS

Whether you are part of a large organization, a small company or a startup, your first step in putting the formula to work is to examine the clarity of your strategic focus. Your strategic health is every bit as important as your financial health. Ask yourself if your strategic limits are clearly defined. Do you have a clear **Ideal Target** (see inside front cover) that keeps you on course? Does everyone in the organization know and understand the company's strategic direction? Do they know what you will NOT do as well as what you will do? Is your strategy yielding the results needed for sustained financial health? Or are you possibly working with an **Anything Goes Target** or one of the **Fuzzy Targets**?

If your answers to the above questions are anything less than absolutely, 100 percent certain, you may need to re-evaluate your strategic plan, clarify and validate your strategy, or develop a new and more focused strategic direction with clear targets and limits.

Developing a Strategic Plan

Strategic planning is a decision-making process that explicitly answers these questions:

1) What business am I really in? What businesses am I NOT in?

2) What are my unique capabilities? What capabilities do I NOT have?

3) What products or services should I offer? What products or services should I NOT offer?

4) Who are my customers? Who are NOT my customers?

5) Where are my customers located? Where are they NOT located?

6) Which customers will I try to reach? Which customers will I NOT try to reach?

7) How will I attempt to reach my customers? How will I NOT attempt to reach them?

8) Why is my chosen market attractive? Why might it NOT be attractive?

9) What type of employees do I need and what type do I NOT need?

The answers to these who, what, where, why and how questions form the basis for an effective strategy. Remember, strategy sets direction, focuses effort, defines the organization, provides consistency, and resolves the big issues so that people can get on with the details. A good strategic plan gets everyone on the same page and aligns them with the same goals. It enables the team to effectively carry out the plan.

How do you know if you need to re-examine your strategy and clarify your targets?

There are many reasons do strategic planning. If you cannot answer all of the above questions easily, then you are a candidate. If your company is growing rapidly or facing rapidly changing market conditions, then you have a compelling need to analyze and re-formulate or re-validate your strategy.

If your products, services, or markets are approaching maturity, you need to reassess your competitive position and consider making strategic adjustments.

An ownership change also raises strategic questions.

If you need to seek new sources of capital or apply for new and larger loans, a well-developed strategic plan will help you sell your idea and give the investors more confidence in your ability to succeed.

If your leadership ranks have had a lot of turnover, strategic planning can be a powerful vehicle for getting everyone on the same page and developing buy-in and team commitment.

In today's market environment, what you cannot do is fail to anticipate and plan.

APPROACHES TO STRATEGIC PLANNING

If you conclude that you need to develop a strategic plan, the next question is, "What kind of strategic planning process should I use?" In my experience, there are really only four approaches to the process of strategic planning. The first two are internally generated, while the subsequent two are externally facilitated.

Approach #1: The Mind of the CEO. This approach is dominant in small startups and closely held small and medium-sized businesses. Everything flows from one person, and the strategy is quite simply as effective or ineffective as the person creating the strategy and setting the limits. The problem with this method is that it often doesn't get out of the CEO's mind and into the minds of the employees. Remember the typical SME strategy: "Sell as much as possible, make payroll and keep the lights on." The guiding target often is of the **Anything Goes** or **Big Fuzzy** variety.

Approach #2: The Self-Facilitated Team. This approach usually develops when the organization has grown large enough for a team of managers to be working for the CEO. The desire now is to include more people in the planning process, but to still approach it as a "do-it-yourself" project. Like the "Mind of the CEO" approach, it is as effective or ineffective as the CEO who facilitates the team, selects the process and influences the outcome. By virtue of the number of people in the planning process, and the lack of clear understanding of the CEO's directions, these are less likely to be **Anything Goes Targets**, but almost always are **Fuzzy**.

Approach #3: The Expert Strategist. This approach is usually employed when there is a crisis of some sort that the internal team can't handle. It may be a turnaround situation, a rapid growth scenario, a market consolidation or an external force that is beyond the capacity of the company to handle alone. The "Expert" is chosen for some specific knowledge or ability that can "fix" the company. Experts charge a lot, and they expect you to do what they tell you to do. This approach will usually shrink a **Big Fuzzy Target** down closer to an **Ideal Target**, but limits are only defined as well as the Expert Strategist employed can make them. This approach produces a good target, but you can do better.

Approach #4: The Professionally Facilitated Process. In this approach, a planning firm with a structured process and a professional facilitator takes the company's managers through a set of decision filters that allow them to codify their own knowledge, clarify their thinking and define their strategic direction. The job of the facilitator is to ask tough questions and provide a talented and independent set of eyes and ears that will keep your team focused, stretch your thinking, push for decisions and mediate conflicting points of view. This helps set mutually acceptable limits, thus establishing Clarity, Choice and Commitment. Result: an **Ideal Target**.

Which approach you use is based entirely on what stage of growth or change your company is in. Consider the issues you are facing, the level of knowledge you and your team have about strategy and the urgency for action.

But whichever approach you choose, NOT choosing to formulate a compelling strategic plan leaves your company at great risk in today's rapidly changing marketplace.

If you have never had any outside help, I recommend starting with number 4, the professionally facilitated process. It will help you know what you don't know, set essential limits, and clarify precisely where you need expert help. It is the shortest distance between two points.

IV. FINAL THOUGHTS

Focus is simply another word for limits. Focus narrows the field of vision and creates a clear target with clear boundaries. It defines what everyone in the organization should be doing and what they should NOT be doing. If you have focus, you don't accept **Anything Goes** or **Fuzzy Targets**.

The formula for effective strategy lies in the Power of NO. You can unleash this power by establishing crystal-clear limits with a high-quality, well-focused, crisply articulated strategic plan. Are you ready to harness the Positive Power of NO?

* * * * * * *

i   Quote from Michael Porter lecture at Edward Jones, January 2000.

ii   Porter, Michael, 2000 Harvard Business School Case Study of Edward Jones.

iii   Teitelbaum, Richard "Edward Jones: The Wal-Mart of Wall Street," Fortune, October 13, 1997, pp 70-72.

iv   Markides, Constantinos C., All the Right Moves, (Harvard Business School Press, 2000), p 4.

v   Hammonds, Keith. "Michael Porter's Big Ideas," Fast Company, March 2001.

vi   Personal interview by Art Kimbrough, May 2001.

vii   National Research Council Report, "Surviving Supply Chain Integration," March 2000.

viii   Markides, 2000.

ix   Personal interview by Art Kimbrough, April 2001.

ABOUT ART KIMBROUGH

Art Kimbrough is a business strategist, entrepreneur, speaker, consultant and author. He is founder of The Art of Strategy, a strategic planning firm focused on helping small and medium-sized enterprises compete effectively in a rapidly changing global economy, and co-founder of ICLogistics, a Web-based supply chain software solution for small and medium-sized businesses.

Art has been a frequent guest on CNN, CNNfn and Business News Network. He was featured on the cover of *Adult Ed Today* magazine in 1999 when he was named one of America's "Hottest Rising Speakers." Art served as a director in the consulting practice of Malcolm Baldrige National Quality award winner Wainwright Industries Inc. Art regularly speaks at corporate meetings and national conferences on strategies for competing in a rapidly changing economy.

THERE SHE GOES AGAIN!
JUST WHEN WE AGREE ON A GOOD DESIGN,
SHE STARTS TWEEKING IT!

CHAPTER IV.

Change:
The Business Constant

Linda Nash

Change has mystified mankind for millennia. The Chinese Book of Changes, the 3,000-year-old I Ching, provided a formula for answering questions posed by change. We continue to write books, create formulas and wrestle with the issues as each successive generation bemoans the rapid increase in the rate of change.

After Gutenberg invented the printing press in 1450, there was no going back. The possibility of universal communication was unleashed. Because literacy evolved slowly, change trickled down at first. The trickle became a stream and now the creations of mankind are a rushing torrent. People and organizations must adjust quickly, often abruptly, and on a major scale. Rapid change is the status quo.

The last 150 years have given us the industrial revolution, airplanes, automobiles, the harnessing of electricity, telephones, transistors, television, computers, nuclear power, the silicon chip, personal computers, cell phones and the Internet. No wonder we all suffer from change whiplash. The world is linked in real time. Information is immediately available to anyone anywhere. The insulation of isolation has been stripped away.

The way it used to be will never be again. Complacency leads to stagnation and vulnerability. Good planning and vigilance must prevail. Limits must be clearly defined and enforced. NO is not for the faint-hearted or indecisive. NO is for the resolute, the committed, the courageous.

People often use what I call "wiggle words." These words, like "try" and "maybe," are what we use when we don't have the nerve or integrity to deal with the truth. They let us off the hook. Instead of saying a polite, "NO, I can't make it to your party," my "I'll try" leaves us both in limbo. When you hear, "Maybe this will work," "Maybe it's safe" or "Maybe I'll get it completed," how much confidence does that engender? Is it Yes or NO? Make a commitment.

Habits of speech betray one's underlying way of thinking. I might not like to hear NO but at least I know where we both stand. It saves me time and lets me move in another direction rather than waiting to see if the "try" or "maybe" works out.

Organizations don't function well on "maybes." Concrete decisions, even if they prove wrong, are better than fuzziness. New Coke is a great example. Coca-Cola was losing market share to Pepsi, and after a series of studies and focus groups, Coke's executives came up with a new product. They committed. They hired Bill Cosby to do television commercials and rolled out an extensive marketing campaign. The product bombed. Less than three months later, the company reintroduced Classic Coke, and market share shot up. Coke survived and thrived. Why? The free publicity was priceless. New Coke was a dud, but it was everywhere. All the stunned lukewarm Coke lovers were jolted into action, grateful to be able to purchase their Classic Coke again.

Where does the power of NO fit? First, Coke was willing to say NO to an old product that had made billions of dollars but seemed not to be working. The company made a difficult decision – a major shift. It committed – not foolishly on a whim, but with strategic research and planning. When the new product failed, Coke had the flexibility and courage to say NO again. Within weeks it had jettisoned the entire marketing campaign, developed new packaging and a new marketing campaign for Classic Coke and had it on the shelves for customers. In both cases the company was crystal clear about the NO and had the capacity to respond quickly.

THREE REASONS FOR CHANGE

Incremental change is a given. But when making a major overhaul or charting a new direction, an organization will have a lot of fallout to contend with. There are three reasons for change: change for the sake of change, change to accommodate and on-purpose strategic change.

Most organizations will say that their change is the strategic kind. Something must be in the drinking water – they're delusional. I've known big-time executives, with degrees from the best business schools, who rationalize reasons one and two. But those types of change can prove devastating and even fatal.

1. CHANGE FOR THE SAKE OF CHANGE

Organizations too often follow the management trend *du jour* into the mire of poor morale, lost intellectual capital, protracted decline in productivity and financial loss. I've been called in to mop up the "blood" more than once. The organizations are stuck in neutral; they suffer long-term damage; and they are vulnerable to unwanted takeovers.

Some reorganizations fall in this category. The success rate for so-called "rightsizing" ranges around 10%. And about one in three mergers is successful. These are glaring rates of failure. Why are the statistics so negative? Among the failures I've witnessed, the reasons for the change weren't clearly defined or the planning and implementation were mediocre at best. The low success rate indicates decisions made without strategic forethought.

If you hear about new ideas, methods, processes, products or organizational structures, by all means evaluate them. But make sure you have a strategic fit. Then, create a definitive plan – and make sure you have the will and resources to implement it. The gurus don't have to deal with your losses. They might even profit from them.

Don't March into the NO Zone

Last year, rummaging through a box of miscellaneous stuff, I discovered an audiotape that a well-known futurist had created almost 10 years ago. I popped it into my car's tape deck to revisit his words of wisdom as I drove to the airport. It was laughable. The laugh was on me. I paid for the tape. Nothing he predicted had happened. Nothing. But it sounded good and many organizations spent thousands, even millions of dollars heeding his words.

The NO Zone is the red ring around a bull's-eye. It's the area that lowers your score; in business, it reduces your bottom line. It is the line you should not cross without strategic reasons.

Well-known companies, some now gone, lost both identity and profits dipping into the NO zone because they thought they could make a few extra bucks.

People Issues

Change for the sake of change has happened in many organizations. Everyone knows it. Employees' first reaction is, "This will blow over. They tried this before. I'll just keep my head down." People drag their feet, productivity slows and so does innovation. Sadly, they are often right. It does blow over, sameness oozes to the surface and valuable time, energy, and money have been wasted. The workers, meanwhile, get the message that real change won't happen to them.

When it is for real and carving begins or processes change, the people react with stunned disbelief. As in a raided anthill, the chaos of trying to survive ensues.

In one organization I worked with, the leaders kept changing directions without strategic reasons. They never informed employees adequately or gave them time to make a transition to new ways of doing things. Turnover was increasing, so the CEO called me to help reduce it. Even when confronted, he and his staff denied the real problem. They mistakenly thought they were forward-thinking and progressive. They progressed – into oblivion.

2. Change to Accommodate

Accommodation change can be small, or it can be sudden and drastic. Small accommodations happen when a company stretches into the NO zone to pick up an extra piece of business. Drastic ones happen in response to a market or economic failure.

Suppose your NO Zone says you won't sell to clients who purchase less than $50,000 a year. But the economy dips and you need cash flow. Will you sell to a client at $45,000? How about $40,000? It will boost your cash flow but could make the borders between your bulls-eye and NO Zone fuzzy for a long time. Most of us have used this strategy occasionally. The danger is that, like the leak in the dike, it will grow. That $45,000 one-time compromise sends a signal and may spiral out of control, creating a company-wide license for exceptions.

Changes made to accommodate drastic situations tend to be too radical unless an organization has done some prudent "what-if" planning. A company that hasn't planned properly tends to overdo the change at first, then retrench later. A company that is prepared for multiple eventualities can respond calmly and quickly. Of course, this goes in the on-purpose strategic change column.

People Issues

If your organization has a defined NO Zone but makes exceptions when business is slow, or when it wants to accommodate a good client, the limits are breached. Once the target has been made fuzzy, people may start testing to assess the size of the breach. They'll be satisfied with making the "easy" sale; they'll come in late; they'll reduce quality. Cultures are based on what is rewarded, what is punished and what is tolerated. Be careful.

3. On-purpose Strategic Change

Obviously, this is the best kind of change and has the greatest chance for success. Clarity is the watchword. Be clear about the Why, the What and the How. Harley-Davidson's successful turnaround is a testament to on-purpose change and Limit Theory™. Founded in 1903, Harley-Davidson was the only motorcycle producer left in the USA by 1953. The company went public in 1965 and merged with AMF in 1969. Ten years later AMF changed strategic direction, a buyout was arranged and Harley returned to private ownership. It enjoyed substantial profits for a few years. But out-of-date designs, high prices, a serious recession and imported look-alikes drove Harley's market share from 90% to 23% over ten years. It lost money for the first time in 50 years.

Harley's management eventually turned the company around by relying on four key principles. First, the company defined its niche as the high-end market. All resources were committed to that segment. Second, a just-in-time system reduced inventories and debt. Third, the company began competing on the basis of value (based on customers' perception), not price. Fourth, Statistical Quality Control was implemented and people were trained and empowered as process owners.[i]

All four principles represent clear limits. Organizations are ultimately defined by what they are not, what they don't or won't do and what they will not tolerate. What remains is a clearly defined **Ideal Target** (see inside front cover). Empowering people as process owners makes them part of the solution. They're accountable and they're responsible for maintaining the focus and the limits.

Failure Costs

Failed change and failure to change both have significant costs. Interestingly, the costs are similar. In both cases, the costs include unsolved problems, missed opportunities, wasted resources, declining morale, loss of job security, loss of intellectual capital, loss of market share, loss of employee confidence in management and a negative bottom line. Your job is to make an informed decision on which way to go and how far to go, and then make it stick.

In Limit Theory™, anything that isn't NO is Yes. Realizing this takes courage and commitment. Don't "yes but" yourself to death. Avoid ambiguity – your organization's future is at stake. Develop your criteria for deciding clearly and unequivocally what is in the NO Zone. If leaders develop fuzzy guidelines, what can you expect from the work force? Has this happened in your organization? What did it cost?

Note: Criteria for change should be tempered by legal and ethical practices and should never be a way to propagate prejudices.

HOW DO YOU MANAGE CHANGE?

Some organizations make change look easy. Others lurch through every pothole and bump in the road. Most are somewhere in between. How you manage change depends on how your organization is defined and the resilience of both the leadership and workforce.

Turn to the inside front cover and look at the five targets. Which one best describes your organization? Are the limits of the red NO Zone clearly defined or fuzzy? Is your yellow target zone so large that anything is acceptable or so small that your organization has an "all the eggs in one basket" philosophy? How "on target" are you? Be honest with yourself – this isn't the time for "maybe" thinking.

Your organizational target is a predictor of both the problems you will face and the methods you should use in managing change.

RESILIENCE

The strength, or resilience, of an organization is an accurate predictor of how long it will take to make changes, and of how successful those changes will be. Resilience comes in three stages, and a company won't be successful unless it is strong in all of them.

The first stage is the Core. It includes mission or purpose, values, collaboration, communication, customer knowledge and service. If this is weak, fix it before you attempt a change. These areas are fundamental to an organization.

The second stage determines Speed. This includes willingness to change, adaptability, creativity, innovation, and risk tolerance. Many organizations have a solid core but get stuck in stage two. Weakness here means a protracted transition.

The third stage determines How High, or how successful you will be. This is the area for new vision, responsibility, implementation and commitment. This is where most organizations concentrate their effort – the moving forward. If your organization is not moving forward at a reasonable pace, check out stages one and two. If they are weak, you won't move much.

Resilience is the ability to bounce back from changes, setbacks, and challenges. The strength of your organization is directly related to the type of target that defines your organization. Using Limit Theory™ (setting crystal-clear limits) will make your organization more resilient by clarifying expectations, targeting use of resources and eliminating wasted motion.

BECOME A MASTER GARDENER

Change is the way all things grow. The master gardener creates a plan based on type of garden desired, climate and available sunlight. She determines the best mixture of soil and fertilizer, carefully selects top-quality seeds or plants and places them strategically for the greatest impact each season. So it is with organizations. The best determine a clear strategy, hire the right people, define the limits, and provide the resources to ensure success.

Even with constant vigilance and care, some plants grow and some do not. The ones that flourish may become overcrowded, drain nutrients from each other and cause stunted growth and poor blooms. Thinning is necessary to insure space, light, and adequate nutrition to the strongest plants. Even good plants often must be discarded in favor of the best.

WEEDING AND THINNING

What most organizations do is maintenance weeding. It reflects small changes. You say NO to bad accounts, ideas that haven't worked and people who perform poorly. Such day-to-day limit enforcement takes care of urgent needs but isn't enough to insure steady growth ·or the great blooms that impact the bottom line.

Thinning is saying a positive NO to things that rob time, sap resources and keep the organization from flourishing in the yellow bull's-eye. Modestly off-target products, ideas or procedures can creep further into the NO Zone, adding fuzziness, stress and a declining bottom line. Thinning can spare an organization from the stunting and slow death of expanding **Fuzzy Targets**, poor choices, and a lack of commitment to organizational strategy.

General Electric Co. is a great thinner. It has a very clear Strategic Operating Principle. If it can't be first or second in a market, GE gets out. Executives water and fertilize but if the product, division, or company doesn't hit the yellow target zone, it is thinned out. No wonder former CEO Jack Welch earned a reputation for being tough. It takes courage to say NO and stick to it.

Southwest Airlines employees are empowered to make suggestions and decisions about weeding, thinning and growing. This is communicated clearly and it is not just lip service. Managing change at Southwest is simply day-to-day management, and the corporate culture fosters communication and commitment. While repeatedly winning awards for on-time performance, baggage handling and customer service, Southwest maintains the lowest employee-to-customer ratio in the industry. When you're clear about the NO, the Yes is easier, less stressful and more profitable. It can be fun, too.

ANYTHING GOES TARGETS

If you work for an **Anything Goes** organization, being "on target" is easy. You welcome any business and will do anything to keep a customer happy, whether it is cost effective or not. After all, money is money, the customer is always right, and you need all the customers you can get. The NO Zone, the red ring around your target, is small, so it doesn't contain many NOes.

As the name implies, an **Anything Goes** organization doesn't focus on much. Nothing is closely checked, quality is whatever happens, resources are splattered about and accountability turns into finger-pointing.

Without competition, the organization may survive. But it will stagnate, bogged down by a sizeable payroll with mediocre to low productivity, overspent resources and a diminishing bottom line.

Many organizations begin with **Anything Goes Targets**. Hopes are high, money is short and the YES and NO Zones are not clearly defined. At first the direction makes sense. The future is wide open, and you begin making money. But like a plastic wind-up toy, the unfocused organization eventually runs into a wall and keeps running in place doing the same thing until it goes belly-up or gets taken over. If this unflattering scenario makes you uncomfortable, it may be pushing your truth button.

Change for an **Anything Goes** organization is painful but necessary. This was true for many U.S. companies as we moved out of the U.S.-dominated 1950s and early '60s and into the more competitive '70s and '80s.

Anything Goes organizations haven't done enough weeding, much less thinning. The first step is to begin shrinking the bull's-eye and clarifying the NO Zone. There are two ways to do it, gradually or total change.

CHANGING THE TARGET

A growing company should steadily clarify and increase the NO Zone. A sharp "we won't go past here" line should form the bull's-eye. As the No Zone gradually increases, a large fuzzy area, a "maybe" zone, a red-yellow area forms." We call this the **Big Fuzzy Target**. There is a plan for the bull's-eye; some definite NOes exist, but exceptions are made arbitrarily.

History and tradition should be honored during any change, Whatever works for the new target zone should be retained, but change requires saying NO to many things: processes, ideas, reporting relationships, organizational structure and physical facilities. Then there are the products, services, clients and, most difficult, the people.

Susan Bishop, author of the Harvard Business Review article "The Strategic Power of Saying No" (HBR, December 1999) and President of Bishop Partners, left a competitive Manhattan executive search firm to follow her dream of running her own executive search consultancy.[ii] She was in a tough market, but knew she could provide better service and better results to clients looking to locate executive talent.

Bishop says: "When we began, our target was larger and somewhat fuzzy, too." Bishop was successful but quickly realized that both time and money could be better allocated. She clarified and narrowed her bull's-eye, increasing the NO Zone. She decided to limit searches to top level executive positions in her core industries. It meant turning down needed business, nearly $250,000 worth, facing fear and sticking to the commitment. It meant that a few valued people had to be let go. Many on her staff were young and eager but without the skills and experience required for the higher level, more exacting, target.

Bishop says, "As a startup we had become like a family. This was extremely painful for me and the company – like a divorce – but it had to be done." Many companies make the mistake of keeping people who are no longer appropriate. Stress increases as they desperately try to meet goals. In many large organizations someone who doesn't meet standards is shoved into a meaningless, killing-time sort of job. Everyone knows it, including them. It's demoralizing, devaluing, and keeps the individual from seeking a more appropriate position – a better fit for career success and fulfillment.

Whatever the size or longevity of an organization, handing out pink slips to employees is unnerving. Even the most jaded managers tense up and feel guilt. Fear is heightened in remaining staff, and survivors' guilt can be a powerful leveler of lofty plans. If the cut is too deep, intellectual capital may be depleted – a costly error. We already know the high failure rate of downsizings, although they temporarily jack up stock prices.

Weighing costs is crucial. Severance packages and outplacement are cheap compared with the cost of missed opportunities, wasted resources and lost market share. Evaluate the long-term impact before making wholesale cuts. Quality people are the most difficult to replace. If you have decided that specific people, departments, or even divisions are in the NO Zone, then do it. Just be sure to provide each individual with a fair safety net. You will feel better, your organization will be perceived more positively and you will minimize the survivors' loss of morale and productivity.

THE IMPACT OF CHANGE

Loss and Letting Go

> "When our first parents were driven out of Paradise, Adam is believed to have remarked to Eve: 'My dear, we live in an age of transition.' "
>
> *William Inge*

All change involves letting go of something. On the personal level it may be a relationship, a place, a habit, an attitude or even that hairstyle from high school. Human beings don't like change because we don't like loss, even when it's good for us. Check out the stuff in your closet, garage or basement for verification. How often have you said, "Oh, well, maybe" and shoved a relic back into the closet instead of saying NO and getting rid of it? We hang on to the past, to what we have, to the known.

Employees who survive a reorganization, especially in a large **Anything Goes** or **Big Fuzzy** organization, will be hurt, angry, and vocal. Not only have you let people go, but now the survivors, dealing with guilt, face a new game and new rules. As you expand the NO Zone and clarify the boundaries, definite limits are imposed. Expectations are changed and accountability is increased. Resistance will occur. Don't over-react.

If you attempt to leap directly from **Anything Goes** or **Big Fuzzy** to **Ideal Target**, the blood will run. If it's too late or too costly to try incremental change this may be the only solution. It will be chaotic. Prepare for significant resistance. Realize that communication is critical. Don't screw up here as most do.

As Pogo says, *"We have met the enemy and he is us."*

REALISTIC TIMELINES

> "The key to everything is patience. You get the chicken by hatching the egg, not by smashing it."
>
> *Arnold Glasow*

Timeline projections are usually too aggressive. People don't change, they transition. New software is change. Mergers are change. New organizational structure is change. But people require time to adjust, understand, mourn losses and let go. They even need time to be angry. The amount of time required will depend on the organization's resilience level and on how effectively the change is communicated and implemented.

As an executive or top-level manager you have probably had months or even a year to understand, plan, and make your own peace with the issues. After an announcement, expect a period of adjustment. Don't be surprised if people don't get with the program immediately. They will be numb with surprise or disbelief.

Do not assume that smiles and nodding heads mean approval. Some people laugh when they're scared to death! Most will be scared, and you may even be one of them. The unknown, even with detailed planning, is a scary thing. Ask anyone who has gotten married.

Before making announcements, develop your timeline. I recommend beginning at the end and working backwards. It provides a different perspective. Borrow the techniques used for marketing and political campaigns. Map your strategy, allowing adequate transition time based on your organizational resilience level.

MAKING THE SALE

EFFECTIVE COMMUNICATION

> "You communicate, you communicate and then you communicate some more. Consistency, simplicity and repetition is what it's all about."
>
> *Jack Welch*

When people are stressed, their hearing goes first. Disruptive news must be communicated often, clearly, directly, and in a timely manner. Even then you'll hear people say, "No one told me." Employees who lack awareness, understanding and acceptance of a strategy can't be expected to enthusiastically commit to carrying it out.

"The biggest problem most companies have during change is communicating too little, too late and too unreliably," says Thomas Lee, president of Arceil Leadership Communications. "Companies need both a culture and an explicit process that together encourage comprehensive, candid communication with their employees. If they want the employees to act like owners they have to treat them like owners."

The company newsletter, intranet, email and voice mail systems all provide information, but acceptance and commitment are often determined by the accessibility and candor of leaders, the way decisions are made, and the humor and discussions around the water cooler.

A manager who has built trusting relationships and leadership credibility with his or her employees will lead more effectively through chaos. Build those relationships now and avoid catastrophe later.

Don't stonewall! If you honestly don't know what will happen or when, tell people that you don't know. Saying nothing communicates dishonesty, intrigue, or downright deceit. No matter what you do, the grapevine will be burning with exaggeration. Be visible and available if you want to pour water on the fire.

Don't do what one executive did. Ed (not his real name) hated that positions had to be eliminated. He really cared. Unfortunately, he lived in another world. In his company the executive parking lot had an executive elevator directly to the ivory tower (they called it the executive floor) containing the lavish, thick-carpeted offices. What would that communicate to you if you worked there?

Ed decided to go to the company plants and be visible, try to explain the situation, and take questions. He wanted workers to think he was one of the guys. Unfortunately, this "guy" wore his $1,000 suit, his $10,000 watch and his sizeable diamond ring. In his defense, he did take off his jacket and roll up the sleeves of his perfectly laundered, monogrammed shirt. His credibility was in the toilet and amazingly he didn't understand why. This is not an isolated case. It can be repeated with a dozen different names. Communication was already bad in this company. The executives just didn't get it.

Ed's company cut too deeply into its knowledge and experience pool, and after four years of trying to stabilize, it was bought out. So was Ed.

Breathe the same air as the people who work for you. Talk with them, not at them. Ed and the rest of the executives certainly communicated a message, but it was the wrong message.

If you know what you want to communicate, then be sure your words and actions are congruent. Build a culture of open, honest communication, paint the crystal clear **Ideal Target**, and you can weather any storm.

SELLING THE WHY

> **"People can live with any 'how' if they understand the 'why.' "**
>
> *Nietzsche*

Sell the "why" before you try to sell the "how." Dumping a "how" onto people and saying, "This is the way it's going to be," won't work. Provide reasons, even if they are painful. "The company has lost sales." "Rolling out the new products is more costly than anticipated." "Projections were way off." "The economy has slumped and we're undercapitalized."

If you're in a growth mode, you may be leaving some good but smaller clients behind to reduce marketing and sales costs, make better use of resources and improve the bottom line. You may be narrowing your focus and getting rid of some fuzziness in your target. Once people understand the "why" and its implications, they are more likely to get on board with the "how."

WHAT'S IN IT FOR ME?

Close on the heels of the "why" question is the "what." What will happen to me? What's in it for me? Facing an unknown is scary. The change may require individual sacrifices for long-term gains. Cutting now may mean greater opportunities later. If this is communicated clearly, acceptance is more likely.

WHAT TO LET GO

Think of sorting through the attic and deciding what to throw out (the junk) and what to keep (the good stuff). This step is almost always overlooked. Organizations are so involved in the chaos and struggling to move forward that they forget about what to let go. It's like trying to drive with the brake on. It also leaves people feeling both emotionally overwhelmed and overworked. I hear it everywhere: "We're trying to do more work with fewer people."

There's a ready answer to such stretched-to-the-limit-rhetoric. In most industries you'll find a few organizations that function well with a lower employee to customer ratio or a lower sales person to sales revenue ratio. They've found a better way, and you can too.

84

> "When faced with the choice between changing and proving there's no need to do so, most people get busy on the proof."
>
> *John Galbraith*

Jack Welch has said, "Only self-confident people can be simple." Insecurity drives us to do many things. We write longer reports than necessary, we create processes and reports that make us look productive and important, and we plan too many time-consuming, unproductive meetings, which cover our backsides and often keep us from the important.

Take a hard look at what can go. What is unnecessary, outdated, unused, cumbersome, time consuming, financially frittering and redundant? Get a big STOP sign. Say NO to this junk so you can say YES to doing the things of real value to your target. You'll save time, money, energy, and angst.

Tell people what they can stop doing before you add to their to-do list. Transitioning from one process to another can require parallel work for a time, but that time should be limited. Give people a deadline so they will understand that this is temporary.

Insure short-term successes. The old saw "nothing succeeds like success" is true. When people are nervous, small successes increase their confidence. Each success increases their ability to take risks – to reach higher.

MAKING THE SHIFT

Listen. Listen to concerns spoken and unspoken. Ask open-ended questions and listen some more. Fear drives people into silence or rebellion, both of which are forms of resistance. People feel vulnerable when they fear losing their self-esteem, position, security or maybe even their house.

Organizations don't like to talk about emotions – after all, this is business. The tendency is to blame the resisters or pretend it's not a problem. I've heard more than one CEO say people just have to buck up or get fired. This is emotional detachment in the extreme. It's avoidance, isolating yourself from the pain. These are the same people who communicate exclusively through memos and email. You never see their eyes.

Managers may use tactics like humor, guilt or peer pressure to erase observable symptoms. While management breathes a sigh of relief, the pain goes underground and the gulf between reality and belief widens.

> **"We usually see only the things we are looking for... so much so that we sometimes see them where they are not."**
>
> *Eric Hoffer, A Passionate State of Mind* [iii]

In bloated bureaucracies, those outdated, multi-layered, traditional organizations, the scenario is slightly altered. The tendency is to become invisible. People get quiet and lie low in hopes that this will pass. Often it does. Long-time employees may be willing to do and tolerate almost anything for the promise of a job and retirement.

Old-style companies create a mindset of dependency. People abdicate their personal career responsibility and view the company as a surrogate parent. After major change, don't count on these people to be highly productive. The world as they knew it is gone.

Transitions take time. People go through emotional stages. Their world is in chaos; they are confused and scared even if they don't express it. If handled properly, the process can move more quickly and the dip in morale can be minimized. People need to feel heard, valued and supported, and they need to feel like they have some influence over their destiny. Provide a way, and make sure it's not just lip service. Active involvement reduces the strain, but nothing eliminates it completely.

Growing Pains – Change and Transition

You started with five people but now you've grown to 100 or 200. You have to change. Rules must be made, jobs are more differentiated and the original five (or 25) are faced with a major transition. A light touch, an open, receptive ear, and an empathetic heart can smooth that transition.

The original group may lose power to the new hotshot CFO and other new talent. There's no time for those fun brainstorming sessions over lunch. You have delegated. The gap between you and the "old guard" is widening, and some don't fit the culture now. They are in the NO Zone. These may be friends who helped you get started and who worked with you side-by-side. You believe you owe them. You do. You owe them honesty and compassion. You owe them a graceful, dignified way out, and you owe them support while they make that transition. The fatal mistake is to do nothing. Say NO, do the right thing, and stick to your target or face stagnation.

A Transition Case

Tom had risen through the ranks of a national company over 25 years. This talented, likeable man performed well, had the trust of the work force and was groomed for the top slot. But he had one problem. Someone on the board wanted to be CEO and had the political clout to get it.

Tom, while greatly disappointed, accepted the situation with mature grace and pledged his loyalty. Two months later, the CEO asked to see him. He agreed that Tom was talented, trusted and doing a fine job. He thanked him for being supportive and for helping smooth the transition. Unfortunately, the loyalty and support Tom had developed through the years was affecting the new CEO's ability to lead. He was honest enough to say to Tom, "They won't follow me while you're still here, so I have to let you go."

What would you have done if you were that CEO? Who should have said NO when? I'll leave you to ponder this one. You may face something similar someday, on one side of the desk or the other.

Change and the Anal Target

The **Anal Target** represents an organization with a large, well-defined NO Zone and a narrow, highly focused Yes Zone. The danger here is rigidity. A major change or shift in the economy, industry or competition could prove lethal. If you own a large share of your niche, maintain awareness of trends, and stay positioned and prepared strategically to expand or change your target, a large NO Zone can work.

Susan Bishop of Bishop Partners says she is moving in this direction. She believes she has an **Ideal Target** now, but she says, "Every year I raise the bar." [iv] While she is crystal clear about her target industries and the financial boundaries, she modifies the target and increases requirements annually for her staff. This may sound cold but it's not. Bishop requires people to get continuing education, but she reimburses them for it. She revisits the organization's mission and values at regular staff meetings and re-evaluates direction and goals with staff twice a year.

There are no surprises. "People know when they are no longer meeting requirements. They know the expectations and their numbers." Bishop has to let some people go, but her company is known for excellent training and she provides strong recommendations, so people easily move to good jobs for which they are more suited.

Change Leadership

Max DePree, former chairman of Herman Miller, says in his book *Leadership Jazz*, "Leader is not always a position. Whatever one's position, the amount of ambiguity involved is directly proportional to the amount of leadership required." [v]

Ambiguity and chaos are part of the transition process. It's the fence-straddling period. One foot is in some nebulous, foggy future and the other is mired in the past. Even the most willing may be confused.

The leader's job is to make sense of the chaos, provide calm direction and support and to guide people to the eye of the storm while navigating to the new shore. Provide communication, interpretation, inspiration, motivation and clear direction. Tell people what is Yes and what is NO.

> **"Everyone thinks of changing the world, but no one thinks of changing himself."**
>
> *Leo Tolstoy*

If transitions are stalling and trust is in meltdown, check your mirror. Whom do you see? The people you lead reflect your leadership style. Don't expect to change others until you change yourself.

Many executives say to me, "We have to get them to change." "Who is them?" is my reply. I'm always impressed when I hear, "What do we need to do to effect change." Then I know it will be a team effort. Word choice betrays thought process.

CHANGE AGENTS

A change agent is another matter. These are the chaos creators. Usually brought in from the outside, these are the people charged with turning an **Anything Goes** or **Big Fuzzy Target** into at least a **Better Fuzzy** or **Ideal Target**. They stir the pot, turn things upside down and become the lightning rod for blame and anger. They usually are placed at the helm but rarely stay long.

Marvin Runyon is such a man. He helped reorganize the Tennessee Valley Authority and then moved on to the United States Postal Service as Postmaster General. Long-time employees knew something was afoot. He was an outsider and his reputation had spread. He wasted no time in creating chaos and soon had the nickname "Carvin' Marvin." The change was painful and prolonged but a new U.S. Postal Service emerged.

We don't like NO people. They tell us what we'd rather not hear – the truth. After the NO people have completed their work, it's often an internal person who takes over to heal the wounds and calm things down. Organizations begin to grow fuzzy again. Complacency is a tough virus to eradicate.

BE VIGILANT

Constant vigilance and full awareness are necessary for course corrections and new choices. Several years ago I asked Chuck Drury, president of the highly successful Drury Inns, "What is your greatest fear?" Without hesitation, he answered, "That we won't be vigilant." Savvy leaders know that drift into complacency or losing clarity about strategic direction will cripple or destroy an organization.

TRANSFORMATION

Transformation is the ultimate goal. It is more than mere change. One kind of energy becomes another. It is the chrysalis becoming the butterfly. It is the dynamic creation of a new way of being, a new way of seeing, a new way of doing. It is a new place, a new level of functioning. It is a new bull's-eye with a crystal clear NO Zone surrounding it.

A transformed organization is one where everyone understands and supports the mission. Leaders are trusted; communication is open and honest. People are valued and empowered to take action. They feel their ownership. It is a WE organization where the energy of responsibility and commitment are palpable. An undeniable spirit permeates the atmosphere. This is the **Ideal Target**.

CONCLUSION

Strategically planned and well-implemented change can transform an organization. Change is painful because it involves losing, giving up something. The amount of pain depends on the quality of the leadership, the way the business has been run (type of target), and the resilience of the work force. In all three areas the key is the ability to strategically set limits and say NO. It is possible to manage change well, but you have to make clear decisions, commit to and communicate a plan of action and then stick to it.

*   *   *   *   *   *   *

i   Sentell, Gerald D., *Fast, Focused, & Flexible*, (Pressmark International), pp 176-180.

ii   Bishop, Susan. "The Strategic Power of Saying No," <u>Harvard Business Review</u>, Nov./Dec. 1999, pp 4-11.

iii Hoffer, Eric, *A Passionate State of Mind*, p 23.

iv   Personal interview by Linda Nash, Sept. 2001.

v   DePree, Max, *Leadership Jazz* (Del Publishing 1992), p 224.

ABOUT LINDA NASH

L inda Nash, MBA, is president of L.J. Nash & Associates Inc., a management consulting, training and research company. She helps organizations nationwide that want to insure optimal success through the chaos of change, transition and transformation.

Clients attest to Nash's in-the-trenches perspective and customized approach to lessening the negative impacts of change and improving performance, commitment and courage. Nash's breakthrough research has resulted in unique tools for measuring strength, identifying sub-par conditions, correcting underlying causes and achieving higher level functioning.

A sought-after speaker, executive coach, and contributor to publications nationwide, Nash is author of four books: *Surviving In The Jungle*, *The Shorter Road To Success*, *Becoming The REAL You and Getting Paid For It!* and *The Bounce Back Quotient*. She is an adjunct instructor at Cornell University in New York and a professional member of the National Speakers Association. She makes her home in St. Louis.

LOOKS LIKE THE COMPANY IS SERIOUS ABOUT THE NEW ETHICAL GUIDELINES AFTER ALL.

CHAPTER V.

Setting Limits:
The Law Does Not Absolve
Us from Thinking

Scott Levine

I am neither an ethicist nor an academic. I don't claim to have all the answers, or even all the questions. But I do make a living counseling business owners on how to run more meaningful and effective enterprises. As a legal advisor, I also help business owners in managing their legal affairs, both business and personal. I have seen how companies are affected by the choices that business owners make. I have concluded that a strong commitment to ethics lies at the foundation of most successful business endeavors. In this chapter, we will explore the relationship between ethics and a business that works.

Laws, by definition, set limits. But when we set out to define our own behavioral limits, it's not sufficient to say, "I'll comply with minimum requirements of all laws and regulations." That isn't a framework for sound decision-making. Laws do not absolve us from having to think. Conduct that is within the law can still be ethically questionable. Recently, it seems that for many business owners, getting through the day without being indicted has been the ethical standard of choice. Avoiding punishment should not be the highest calling for business.

Rather, setting a high ethical standard will help your company survive and succeed by giving it the freedom to focus on its strategies and products. Establishing ethical limits helps managers and employees at all levels understand what is minimally expected of them, and can inspire company-wide clarity and cooperation.

> **"There is a big difference between what we have the right to do and what is right."**
>
> *Hon. Justice Potter Stewart, Associate Justice,*
> *U.S. Supreme Court, 1958-1981.*

WHAT ARE WORKPLACE ETHICS?

Ethics are standards that can guide behavior in the workplace by establishing the limits of acceptable conduct. Typically, employers try to hire people who they assume are ethical people *outside* the workplace. Far less frequently, however, do employers seriously consider compatibility with company policies and practices that generally define acceptable or unacceptable behavior *within* the organization. Most often, the ethics of a business are determined at a high level by the key stakeholders. Unethical workplace behavior can be triggered by overly aggressive financial or business objectives, deadline pressure, competitive threats, real or perceived threats to an organization's survival, attempts to save jobs in the short run, or a simple rationalization that "others do it."

Common unethical acts include lying to supervisors, falsifying records, alcohol and drug abuse, conflict of interest, stealing and receiving gifts or entertainment as *quid pro quo*. Many employers do not regulate these things.

Whatever the cause, the unethical employee takes what would be an **Ideal Target** (see inside front cover) and expands it, under duress, into an **Anything Goes Target**, or at best, one of the **Fuzzy Targets**.

The key influences on ethical workplace behavior are things like personal values, supervisor influence, senior management influence, internal drive to succeed, performance pressures, lack of punishment and the influence of friends and co-workers.

WHY BUSINESS ETHICS?

In short, many of the things that influence workplace behavior are absolutely within the control of the employer. Why, in so many cases, do employers resist setting strong ethical limits and settle for reciting laws as the limit for controlling behavior?

First, many employers do not know how to begin implementing company-wide, integrity-based, business practices based on well-defined ethical limits, nor do they understand the costs of such a change. With any change in business practice, there is an unknown cost associated with the disruption. Many employers are protective of their "culture" to the point where they guard against changing it in any material way. However, it's easier than you think (more on this later).

Second, many companies fail to realize how much better business (and life) works when good ethics guide behavior. Integrity is a critical ingredient for success. There is a famous story involving Mahatma Gandhi. An Indian woman traveled for two weeks, on foot, to meet this great man. She had a son who was addicted to sugar and sought Gandhi's counsel. When she arrived, she said, "Gandhi, I have traveled for two weeks to meet with you. Please, tell me how to help my addicted son." He replied, "Come back in two weeks." The woman was beside herself but, nevertheless, followed Gandhi's guidance. When she returned in two weeks, he offered her the guidance she was seeking. But she had to ask, "Gandhi, why did you make me wait two weeks after I traveled such a long distance to meet with you?" His reply was simple: "Two weeks ago, I was addicted to sugar." Successful business leaders operate from a base of integrity. Ask yourself, if you don't behave with integrity, why should your employees follow your lead?

Third, many business owners don't understand the costs of unethical behavior or the benefits of ethical decision making. In an Ethics Officer Association Survey, 48% of employees indicated that they had done something unethical or illegal in the past year. These acts included cheating on an expense account, discriminating against coworkers, paying or accepting kickbacks, forging signatures, trading sex for sales and looking the other way when environmental laws were violated. Unethical or illegal acts by U.S. employees cost their employers $400 billion annually.

BUSINESS ETHICS FOR PERSONAL REASONS

It doesn't take a survey to conclude that most individuals would rather work for an ethical employer. It just feels better when we can marry our professional talents and activities with our desire to be better people. For example, many law firms historically have not promoted *pro bono* activity among their staffs. Recently, however, our firm formed a committee to determine whether there would be an interest in identifying volunteer opportunities outside the office and opportunities to do *pro bono* legal work in the office. To gauge interest, an e-mail "trial balloon" was sent to the staff. Nearly 100% of the staff responded positively and enthusiastically. Many people are searching for more meaning in their lives. Employers should not assume that this stops at the office door. If people work at a place where ethical decision-making is not only the norm, but is championed and celebrated, they will feel better about their employer and about themselves.

THE VALUE OF A GOOD REPUTATION

Remember when Mitsubishi used to be known for making cars (instead of sexual harassment indictments brought by the EEOC in 1996)? How about Exxon for selling gasoline (as opposed to protecting drunken oil tanker pilots in 1989)? Arthur Andersen for world-class consulting services (Enron…need we say more)? Once a company or its employees make poor ethical choices, the company carries the baggage of those choices despite successful and sincere efforts to reform. The absurdity of allowing poor ethical activity is compounded by the fact that these companies spend millions of dollars developing their image and reputation. All of this can be undone by one bad decision.

Firms that adhere to ethical standards perform better financially over the long run. A 1997 study on the relationship between corporate behavior and financial performance looked at firms whose unsafe products led to regulatory or criminal violations or product liability litigation. These firms experienced lower returns and slower sales growth even five years after their safety lapses occurred.[i]

The Tylenol tampering incident of 1982 offers one of the most telling examples of the rewards of being ethical. When Tylenol capsules were discovered to have been tainted with deadly poison, Tylenol's manufacturer, McNeil Consumer Products Company, a subsidiary of Johnson & Johnson, followed its code of ethics, which required it to put the interests of the consumer first. In what many financial analysts and economists considered to be a disastrous decision and a dreadful mistake, McNeil recalled all Tylenol capsules – 31 million bottles with a retail value of about $100 million. A new and safer caplet form of Tylenol was developed, and within a few months Tylenol regained its majority share of the market. The recall turned out to be neither a poor decision nor a financial disaster. Instead, the company's actions enhanced its reputation and created a bond of trust and respect between Tylenol and customers.

Unethical behavior, on the other hand, often has disastrous results. For example, defense contractors that were part of the spending and overcharging scandal several years ago are still reeling from the charges and struggling to regain credibility. The Beech-Nut baby food company suffered tremendous losses as a result of the revelation that its "apple juice" contained neither apples nor juice. Consumer groups began boycotting Nestle in the early 1970s over its intense marketing of infant formula in Third World nations, where a lack of sanitation, refrigeration and education led to serious health problems in formula-fed infants. In 1989, nearly 20 years after the first boycotts, Nestle found that consumers were slow to accept its new "Good Start" formula. The boycott was still under way, and continues in many forms today. Like an individual's reputation, a firm's reputation for ethical behavior takes a long time to build, can be lost instantly as the result of one bad choice, and can be almost impossible to recover.

In 1992, Texaco was rocked by the disclosure of tape-recorded conversations among three executives about a racial discrimination suit. The lawsuit, filed on behalf of 1,500 employees, alleged a pattern of discrimination by Texaco as well as a hostile environment. The tape-recorded conversations, although subsequently established as containing errors, quoted one executive (accurately) as saying, "I'm still having trouble with Hanukkah. Now, we have Kwanzaa. (Laughter)." A boycott against Texaco was declared, and the company's stock price fell $3. Within days, Chief Executive Peter Bijur pledged to eliminate discrimination and settled the discrimination suit for $176 million. His pledge ended the boycott and restored both earnings and stock value.

As we all know, such behavior is not confined to large corporations. For example, a client recently contacted me about a lawsuit he wanted to bring against a former sales employee. My client is a well known software developer. The former employee left to work for a competitor and was siphoning customers away from my client. That employee was bound by a non-compete clause in an employment agreement. I reviewed the agreement and advised my client that he had a strong case. The contract was ironclad and the violation was clear. It was my opinion that a judge would uphold the employee's obligations under the contract and compel him not to compete for some period of time.

As a courtesy, I forwarded a copy of the lawsuit we prepared to the former employee with a cover letter advising that I would be in court in a few days seeking an injunction to compel him to stop working for the competitor. The next day, I received a call from a local lawyer advising that he would be representing the former employee in the lawsuit my client was going to file. The dialogue proceeded:

Employee's Attorney: *"Does your client (the employer) really want to file this suit?"*

SL: *"I wouldn't have sent the letter if he didn't."*

Employee's Attorney: *"Given the circumstances of his leaving, I would think your client (the employer) would not want to have a public discussion about it."*

SL: *"I was under the impression your client (employee) quit without notice."* (If an employer terminates an employee, it is difficult to maintain a cause of action for injunctive relief under the basic theory that, if the employee was so important to your business, you wouldn't have terminated him. It wouldn't be fair, according to the legal principle, to prevent him from working for a competitor when he cannot continue to work for your company, either).

Employee's Attorney: "*Well, according to my client (employee), your client (employer) fired him because he wouldn't comply with a demand that he falsely manufacture a document that was to be used to assemble a bid on a software development project.*"

SL: "*That's news to me. I'll look into it and get back to you.*"

My client's explanation was that it was the local industry practice to "inflate" the numbers for work to be performed by subcontractors. The subcontractors would be paid one amount but the bid would be for a larger amount. This enabled the general contractor to have larger profits. It was the accepted practice, according to my client. While he denied that he asked his employee to do anything illegal or unethical, he did not deny the practice.

He dropped the case. Why? Because he was concerned that in a deposition or trial, he would be forced to testify about his business practices. That could provide his competitors with an advantage and cause his clients to question his business practices. It could be devastating to his business.

Even though the suit was never brought, the consequences were significant. Word on the street was that you could hire away my client's sales staff because he would not (or could not) enforce his agreements. His sales people are less inhibited by the restrictions of their agreements because they all know of his business practices. In short, his unethical business practices have exposed his company to his competitors in a way that could have critical consequences for his business.

Poor ethical choices can result in tremendous financial setbacks for a company – even, in the case of Enron, destruction. The right core values, on the other hand, can help a firm achieve longstanding profitability. The Crown Candy Factory offers some insight into longevity, profitability and values.

When I was a child, my parents would take me to an old-fashioned soda fountain in North St. Louis called Crown Candy Kitchen. This shop has not changed a bit since I was a child and, as far as I can tell, looks much like it did when it opened nearly 80 years ago. Its success has spanned generations, and today people come from miles around to sample the handmade chocolates, homemade ice cream and giant banana malts. This business has never experienced a "paradigm shift" or "synergy" and likely has no use for such buzzwords, but it recognized its strength and stuck with it. Through the proliferation of everything from the shopping mall to McDonald's, Crown Candy has never changed. The owners know their business, know their strengths and never forgot their roots. This is the best framework for an ethical workplace and it is simple.

Ethics in business is not simply something nice to do if you can afford it. If a firm behaves ethically, it can generate good will that can help through the difficult times. Without such good will and trust, a firm can be destroyed. Investors, consumers and employers may turn away from a company that behaves unethically. In the cases of Enron and Arthur Andersen, such conduct was fatal.

Leadership's Role in Ethical Choices

Most business law controls business conduct in an area where there was once no control but, rather, the opportunity for businesses to self-regulate by making good ethical choices. For example, before requirements were imposed by Congress and the Securities Exchange Commission, companies had the option of designing their own investment offerings that protected the rights of the "least sophisticated" investor. Because too few companies did so, we now have a full – and costly – set of regulations. More recently, in many states, the problems resulting from the overzealous use of telemarketing have resulted in regulation.

Ethical choices afford firms opportunities to take positions ahead of the curve. Firms can choose to go beyond the law and perhaps avoid regulation that might be costly or litigation that can be devastating. Take, for example, the story of an angry ex-employee, Rhonda Pelts.

Rhonda Pelts was employed by Midwest Sales, Inc. ("Midwest") as an accounts receivable clerk. Her job was to contact customers and collect past-due accounts. The office atmosphere at Midwest was somewhat loose. All employees, both male and female, told off-color stories, played practical jokes on one another, often with sexual content, and engaged in ongoing banter of a personal nature. After about one year, Pelts began to sour on her job. The Midwest president and office manager warned her several times about her attitude, but they didn't document these warnings. One day, two other employees saw Pelts go to the president's office, open the payroll envelope and review employees' paychecks. When told of this, the Midwest president and office manager met and decided to terminate Pelts. During the termination meeting, Pelts left the office in tears. The following day, Midwest received a letter from Pelts' doctor advising that she needed two weeks' medical leave. Two weeks later, Pelts called to say she was returning to work. The Midwest president told her that she had been terminated two weeks earlier and that the decision was final.

Pelts filed claims and received Right to Sue letters from the Equal Employment Opportunity Commission. She sued Midwest, alleging that she was terminated because of her age and because of her opposition to the sexual harassment she endured. Midwest denied these claims. The Federal District Court ordered mediation, which was unsuccessful. Pelts demanded $150,000, where Midwest reluctantly offered a maximum of $25,000. The case resumed and discovery was extensive. Midwest obtained statements from most of Pelts' co-workers, all of which stated that she participated fully in the sexual stories, practical jokes and personal banter. Pelts collected statements from two former female Midwest employees that corroborated her claims of the highly-charged sexual nature of the Midwest workplace and supported her contention that she had complained to management about the environment. A seven-day jury trial resulted in a verdict for Midwest. Did Midwest really win? After two years of litigation at a cost of $275,000, finger-pointing among shareholders and low morale among staff, the answer is a resounding "maybe." Midwest's leadership failed to make a number of choices that could have avoided this conflict:

- It chose not to run a tight ship. What may appear to be good-natured fun, particularly off-color stories, practical jokes and personal banter, may provide substantial ammunition for an unhappy former employee.

- It chose not to train its employees. Pelts' counsel made much at trial of the fact that Midwest provided no employment law training for its managers with regard to discrimination and sexual harassment.

- It chose not to document personnel files carefully. Pelts' file contained no written documentation of her performance reviews or the warnings given for her poor attitude.

- It chose not to provide a formal mechanism to resolve employee complaints. Although Midwest had a policy concerning sexual harassment, no records were kept of employee complaints, investigations of such complaints or resolution of complaints.

Ethical leadership gives businesses the freedom to make choices that can keep them out of the thicket of governmental regulation and the courts. Ethical lapses, as in the Midwest case, leave businesses with less flexibility and increased exposure.

THE POSITIVE POWER OF NO

> "Contemplating any business act, an employee should ask himself whether he would be willing to see it immediately described by an informed and critical reporter on the front page of his local paper, there to be read by his spouse, children and friends."
>
> *Warren Buffett*

Every organization should have a code of ethics, a formal statement of what the organization expects in the way of ethical behavior and of what behaviors are unacceptable, an **Ideal Target** with crystal clear limits between the two. The code must reflect senior management's organizational values, rules and policies and enable self-governance and responsible conduct in accordance with them.

The Positive Power of NO can help you put an integrity-based code into effect. But you must keep this key principle in mind:

The guiding values and commitments must make sense, must be the product of collaboration and must be clearly communicated.

Your company's **Ideal Target** should be defined by clear limits on behavior beyond which you and your company will not go. Unethical conditions should never be allowed to exist out of thoughtlessness. The ethical implications of every work process should be challenged. Again, staying within the law isn't good enough. Your written, spoken and unspoken policies should clearly reflect the bull's-eye you establish to strategically and ethically guide your organization.

Involve your employees in the process. This will allow for buy-in, at every level, to the principle that individuals whose behavior falls outside the limits (like an arrow landing in the red ring) will not be tolerated. Consequences for "out of limit" behavior must be specified and consistently applied, lest the unspoken standards belie the desired standards. A lack of clarity or a low level of accountability means accepting or even promoting a **Fuzzy Target**, and that can be hazardous to your organization's health.

In addition to establishing an **Ideal Target** for acceptable conduct, the organization should establish systems and structures that support this goal. Engage your staff in the development of a system that allows good ethics to be considered in the decision-making process.

The mechanics of the system should be distributed both internally and externally. Management should help employees understand its details and importance. It should clearly specify management's role, make employees responsible for understanding the system and establish a grievance procedure to deal with complaints. Finally, you should survey your employees frequently about the system and be willing to make adjustments as necessary.

- Company leaders must be personally committed to the system and willing to hold everyone accountable for its implementation.

Once your limits are in place, you must be willing to tout successes and strongly condemn failures. The "ethically aware" should be acknowledged at all levels. A high level of commitment from the top can keep an **Ideal Target** from migrating to a **Fuzzy Target**. If you let significant violations occur without consequences, you're sending a strong message that undermines the company's efforts to be more ethical.

Remember that your employees are watching. Be careful not to reward unethical behavior that has a good result. For example, take the case of a lawyer who "holds back" information pertaining to a settlement of a dispute in order to manipulate his client into the "zone of settlement." He would tell his client something like, "I think they will pay $10,000 to settle this dispute" when he already had an offer for $12,000 from the other party. When he would ultimately settle the case for $2,000 more than his client expected, he would receive praise from the client, which, in turn, favorably impacted his position in his law firm. Senior management knew of the practice. However, since the results were positive (client satisfaction equaled timely payment and referrals), the attorney was rewarded rather than being reprimanded. His co-workers, seeking to also gain favor within the firm, also began to cut corners and manipulate clients into settlements. Ultimately, the firm was reprimanded by the Supreme Court for its tactics, and eventually it broke apart.

How often will you be involved in adjudicating infractions? How many of your managers do you want to seek your advice when ethical questions arise? The correct answers are "never" and "none." That's why you hire managers. Your managers must know exactly what is expected, not only within any given department, but within the organization as a whole.

The consequences of behavior outside acceptable limits (red ring) must be clear. Your managers must be empowered to exact consequences when these limits are ignored. If all managers recognize that it is their responsibility to say "NO," the organization will be one that respects ethical limits. Not only must your managers demand action within the **Ideal Target**, they must behave in accordance themselves.

Are workplace ethics a serious subject at your company? Or are they something that you assume and sometimes joke about? If the answer is the latter, it is time to put the Positive Power of NO to work for you and your business. Start with a conversation with your management and staff. Then, start building the systems to help establish a sustainable, long-term commitment to workplace ethics. Remember: It takes a conscious effort to have your business be an authentic representation of your core values. Get started today!

*   *   *   *   *   *   *

i   Milissa S. Baucus and David A. Baucas, "Paying the Piper: An Empirical Examination of Longer-Term Financial Consequences of Illegal Corporate Behavior," 40 Academy of Management Journal 129 (1997).

FIND THE RIGHT TALENT
FOR THE RIGHT JOB

CHAPTER VI

Appreciation²: Applying Power of NO Principles to People Stewardship

Hank Epstein

Have you ever thought about what makes people unique among your organization's resources, such as equipment or raw material or even systems? Over time equipment loses value, it depreciates on the books. Your brand-new automobile may lose 25% of its value when you drive it off the dealer's lot. Most materials have a shelf life. If you don't use them in a timely fashion they become unusable. Try opening a carton of cottage cheese a week or two after its "purchase by" date and the smell will make my point. Systems also become obsolete over time. Remember what it was like to file documents in the old DOS PC operating system? How does that compare with the ease of using Windows Explorer® to perform the same task?

While inanimate resources all lose value over time, people are the only resource you have with the potential to appreciate. Notice that I said potential. In many organizations, people are treated no differently than machines. They are given orders without understanding why. They are laid off and reinstated as one might flip a machine's on/off switch. They are worked relentlessly with no thought for their families or other obligations, roles, and interests outside the workplace. When we treat people like machines, they depreciate like machines. You know the signs of human depreciation. Absenteeism, low morale, shoddy workmanship and zero loyalty are just a few of the symptoms. In this chapter we will explore the connection between your **appreciation** of your human resources and their **potential for appreciation.** I like to call it the **Appreciation^2** (Appreciation Squared) effect.

Twenty years of research by the Gallup organization has revealed that workers who feel appreciated have a higher level of engagement with the work they do. Organizations that have broken the code to getting their workers engaged have been able to generate upwards of 50 percent more profit growth than organizations that haven't, AND they are able to sustain this growth in weak as well as robust economies.[i] So what is engagement and how do you produce it?

Customers can easily recognize engagement. It's the waiter who steers you away from a menu item because it doesn't look good to him in its raw state. It's the airline pilot who keeps you informed of the causes and expected duration of traffic and ground delays so you don't wonder why you're still sitting at the gate 30 minutes after the scheduled departure time. It's the checker at the grocery store that reminds you there is a two-for-the-price-of-one special on an item you bought. An engaged worker relates to her job as if she owns it. She takes pride in knowing what to do and has a knack for doing it well. She relates to her colleagues as customers and takes the time to learn how to satisfy them with the goods she produces or the services she provides. She enjoys what she does and derives a deep sense of satisfaction and fulfillment from it.

Not surprisingly, the Gallup research also confirms what many of you have felt instinctively for years. The single largest determining factor in having a worker own his work is the quality of the one-on-one relationship he has with his boss. In short, **Appreciation^2** is a function of boss mastery.

Power of NO principles can help you create a sense of ownership both in the executive suite and on the factory floor. The performer (a word I will use instead of worker to indicate the applicability of these ideas to all levels of the organization) and the boss need sharply defined domains of account-ability and authority if the organization is to generate **Appreciation[2]**.

STOP STAFFING...START CASTING

Turnover is rampant. Overtime costs are going through the roof. Su-pervisors are screaming for more people to meet the ever-increasing order promise and product quality demands being placed upon them. No won-der you feel compelled to fill open positions with any body your HR department can find. But what price are you paying?

Attracting, hiring and training a worker or manager can cost one year's compensation or more. And these are just the VISIBLE costs. A shop floor or office full of rookies places morale-depressing demands on the veterans who try to cover for them. A rookie mistake can delay a cus-tomer order or dead-end a request for information. Will the customer go elsewhere, and at what loss in revenue? The INVISIBLE costs of unwise hiring can be several multiples of the cost to simply fill an open position.

Appreciation[2] begins with selection and/or promotion. Master Bosses select and promote based upon talent, not skills or knowledge. There's not much energy left to appreciate someone whom you've been micro-managing because his or her capabilities don't match the requirements of the job. In addition, without some knack for doing a job, it is very un-likely that the performer will grow and develop. The performer won't appreciate because the motivation and confidence just aren't there.

Talents are attributes that come with the worker. They are qualities of physical and mental dexterity, habits or behavior and temperament that make the worker unique. When taught skills and given experience, a tal-ented person can perform extraordinarily. Willie Mays, the legendary center fielder for the San Francisco Giants, could run fast and catch well. That's skill. He knew where to stand in the outfield in any game situation and with any particular batter at the plate. That's experience. But his unique homing instinct, triggered by the sound of bat against ball, was what enabled him to track down fly balls that would have gone as extra base hits against other outfielders. That's talent!

The search for talent in the workplace begins by looking at a job from the perspective of what it takes to delight customers. I'm sure you can recall a time when you've been delighted by a talented worker. I am fortunate to know a skilled mechanic who specializes in working on Nissan vehicles exclusively. His expertise is a key reason why I drive only Nissans. Wes can troubleshoot an engine fault and find exactly the correct fix in a few minutes. His work gives me piece of mind with all my vehicles and has saved me untold expense on replacement parts that don't cure the problem. He delights me!

When you have a position to fill, talk to the internal or external customers it serves. Find out when they were delighted last and what happened to produce that feeling. Get specifics. Then ask them when they were disappointed and what caused their disappointment. The answers to these questions will begin to reveal the talents required for outstanding job performance. Will a customer service rep steeped in product knowledge and problem solving skills who takes every nasty remark personally be able to delight an irate customer? I doubt it. Will the meticulous bank teller, possessed of superior numerical skills, delight customers who have 30 minutes during Friday's lunch hour to cash their payroll checks? Probably not. Talent scouting begins with the customer.

Benchmark Your WORST as Well as Your BEST Performers

Now that you have a picture of what outstanding performance looks like, your next task is to learn what qualities in the performer produce that outcome. To do this, pay attention to your BEST and your WORST. Observe how your BEST deal with challenges, influence others, cope with multiple goals and deadlines and react to imposed rules, regulations, and procedures. Notice if they are driven by a need to lead, influence or maintain control; a strong desire to serve others; a concern for achieving a return on the resources they expend; or an intense interest in getting answers or building their expertise. Talk to them about their most challenging situations and listen to how and why they responded as they did. Recognize them for specific outcomes and ask them to share what it was they did that produced that outcome. Do the same with your WORST. They're still on your payroll and they're an excellent source for documenting characteristics you do *not* want to replicate.

Supplement your observations and conversations with a formal analysis of the BEST and WORST performers' behavioral styles and the values that drive those styles. A variety of useful instruments are available, including the DISC model.[ii] The key is to concentrate on measuring how people behave and why they behave as they do rather than measuring aspects of their personality. The idea is to examine the patterns of behavior in the BEST and WORST performing segments of the population we are benchmarking. By comparing the patterns we can identify specific elements of behavior that are associated with success, those associated with mediocrity, and those which are performance neutral.

Give Candidates an Authentic Opportunity to Say NO

Having identified the behavioral dimensions associated with success and mediocrity, we are now in a position to screen job candidates with discipline and consistency. Behavioral research suggests that people hired based only upon their resume combined with an interview have a 14% chance of succeeding in the job and sticking with the organization. When selection is based upon the kind of talent matching process we are describing, the probability of success and retention increases to 75%.[iii]

First, administer a behavioral style instrument to each candidate and compare their results to the success profile. Invite anyone with a reasonable match for an interview. Many selection interviews are conducted more like a sales pitch than a true evaluation interview. This is often due to lack of training and the resultant discomfort the interviewers feel with the interview process. More recently, given the scarcity of candidates in our tight labor market, the interviewer may even be fearful of losing the "body" if she is too assertive.

Use an evaluation interview approach with carefully crafted, behaviorally focused questions that compel the candidate to demonstrate the key talents you have identified in their response. Begin the interview with a description of the talents required to do the job and the most challeng-

WHAT we expect and HOW those expectations are realized. **Account-ability** is what outcomes we hold people to account for.

Our job as Bosses is to make our expectations crystal clear. The familiar acronym SMART provides a template for setting and communicating sharp **Ideal Targets** for what we want from a performer.

Specific: Which outcomes are acceptable, which ones are unacceptable and which ones are we indifferent toward? If I'm a basketball player, I've got to get the ball through the hoop to add value to the team. Rimming the basket or caroming off the backboard may be close outcomes but they don't earn the cigar.

Measurable: What does a quality outcome look like? Within what measurable limits does a quality outcome fall? You may want your customer service reps to handle 20 calls an hour. You also want the customer problem handled in a single transaction if at all possible, so number of call backs are a negative. Your performance measurement might be the difference between calls handled and call backs.

Ambitious: We want performers to be challenged by the outcomes we ask them to produce. Master Bosses view their expectations as a key driver of the performer's growth and development. Your crack salesman is doing a super job of selling the existing product line. Now you want him to learn about new product introduction, so you ask him to make some calls with the R&D director to collect feedback on a new product idea and analyze the implications for the entire product line.

Reachable: We don't want performers to be overwhelmed by the outcomes we ask them to produce. Master Bosses align their expectations with the capabilities of their Performers so that they are stretched but not broken by the outcome targets. Our super salesman may have little or no experience with new product development, but we can provide him with a researcher, applications tester and an advertising copywriter to help him perform the analysis. Now his skills as a team leader are also tested as part of the development opportunity.

Time-bound: Performers need to know precisely when the outcomes are expected. The focus group report that arrives a day after the key meeting to design the advertising campaign isn't very useful. Timing is everything in the creation of an outstanding business enterprise.

Once we have defined our expectations in SMART terms, we have earned the right to hold our performers accountable for those outcomes. Anything less meticulously defined puts us at risk of disappointment and them in a state of uncertainty. Accountability, when it is established in a thoughtful and comprehensive manner by a Master Boss, is not a burden but a source of pride, meaning and satisfaction for a performer with the talents to do the job. Accountability supports ownership.

Now that the WHAT has been addressed, we can examine the HOW. This is more complex because there are myriad ways for the performer to accomplish what we expect. If we want her to exercise maximum free will in execution, we have to provide some parameters and limits within which to exercise her **authority**. How often have you heard a colleague or subordinate complain about not having enough authority to get the job done? By failing to set sharp **Ideal Target** limits on the Performer's unilateral actions, we subvert his freedom to act like an owner. Fuzzy authority limits provide a ready-made excuse for avoiding ownership.

Authority limits can be set in two ways. (1) You may prohibit specific actions, such as not allowing a supervisor to hire any additional people, or not letting a salesperson promise a delivery date without checking with the master scheduler in operations. (2) You may place limits on allowable actions, telling the sales manager he can't spend more than $20,000 on advertising to achieve the sales goal, or the operations manager she can't use more than 15% overtime to fill those orders. Sharp authority limits provide the performer with a lot of freedom to make choices about how to get the job done without continually calling on you, the Boss, to make distracting and time-consuming decisions. Sharp authority limits give the performer **one hundred percent response-ability**.

In an **Appreciation²** culture there is no limit to individual response-ability. In fact, the degree to which any Performer is **able to respond** to people, situations and circumstances that stand between him and the outcomes he is accountable to accomplish, is a measure of the extent he has appreciated as a performer. **One hundred percent response-ability** is the ultimate in empowerment. If I am free to respond to anything that stands between me and what I'm accountable for, within the limits placed on my authority, my free will is maximized. This is a very energizing and motivating place for performers to be. It unleashes their creativity to devise responses to accomplish their goals. It calls forth all the discretionary effort they can muster, and discretionary effort is the Holy Grail that all high-performing organizations are seeking.

YOU OWN THE ENVIRONMENT...THEY OWN THE WORK

We've seen how Power of NO principles can define the limits of job accountability and authority, and how this contributes to job ownership in an **Appreciation²** culture. Now let's use these same principles to distinguish the environment in which the work gets done. In other words, let's see how the Power of NO can define the boss's role in the enterprise.

Master Bosses are talented environmental stewards. They allow the performers to do the work and they assume ownership for the environment. As the owner of the environment, the boss must pay attention to the messages she is sending, both consciously and unconsciously, with her behavior. Saying NO to messages of depreciation and embracing messages of appreciation is crucial to creating job ownership.

Years ago, I worked for a vice president of a Fortune 100 Corporation who proclaimed his commitment to participatory management. He made a point of telling my colleagues and me that he didn't want any yes-men on his staff. "You don't have to worry about me," I eagerly said to myself. The first time I publicly challenged one of his decisions, albeit with grace and respect, I found myself in the doghouse. He transferred me out of his division with mind-boggling speed. The disconnect between his words and his behavior led me to surround myself with a thick protective cocoon of cynicism and to agree with all the pronouncements of my new boss, while biding my time until I could leave the company to start my own business. My value to the organization depreciated substantially and when I resigned it lost the 25 years and hundreds of thousands of dollars it had invested in my professional development, as well as the multimillion-dollar annual contribution made by the products from the new-product development effort I directed.

The Work Environment

What constitutes the work environment? There are three elements:

1. The systems that have been devised, either consciously or by default, for getting the work done.

2. The HR policies and practices that are used to control, reward, and punish worker behavior.

3. The day-to-day treatment the worker receives from the boss.

We'll address each element but, as you might guess, Boss behavior is by far the most critical.

Systems

The continuous-improvement movement fathered by Dr. Edwards Deming has awakened western business culture to the importance of systems thinking. Its core tenet asserts that "all work is a process that can be continuously improved." [iv] The implications of this notion link very closely to the Master Boss' primary objective, which is allowing performers to take ownership of their work.

All business enterprises are organized along hierarchical military lines. In the military, the principal objective is to control the movement of troops on the battlefield (see Figure 1). In a typical configuration, departments are headed by vice presidents who ultimately report to the supreme commander, a president or chief operating officer. But in reality, the work that ultimately delivers the product or service to the customer flows across departmental boundaries. Many successful handoffs are required to produce a deliverable that delights the customer, and departmental boundaries often thwart those handoffs. The result is an experience for the customer that is less than delightful, to say the least.

It's relatively easy to establish ownership for tasks that occur totally within a single department. The challenge that Master Bosses face is to establish and support ownership for the more extensive processes that cross departmental boundaries. A draftsman in engineering can be given clear ownership for the preparation of the drawings required to manufacture the block of an automobile engine. His accountabilities might include obtaining clear specifications from the design department and confirming readability of the drawings with the casting department. It's a far more complex endeavor to assign ownership for the process of assembling the engine. A host of individual components from various departments and even external vendors must be brought together in the right place at the right time and connected properly so that when the assembled device is connected to a fuel source and the ignition switch is activated, the engine fires up.

Master Bosses pay attention to complex ownership issues and engage the performers, who may actually know more than they about the process details, to help with their resolution. They recognize that interdepartmental turf battles are really crises of process ownership. These battles must be resolved to ensure that the supply chain can fill orders with the speed and accuracy that a competitive environment demands.

In addition to the macro issue of process ownership, Master Bosses also pay attention to the micro-issue of process capability. Have you ever had a job where the information you needed was not available in a timely fashion or the equipment you used to accomplish your tasks was shoddy and poorly maintained? If you did, I'm guessing that you were often frustrated and stressed out, especially if your Boss was a demanding, no-excuses sort of guy. Have you ever worked hard on a report that you understood to be a critical deliverable of your job, only to find out that most of the recipients read little or none of it and even wondered why they were receiving it? If you did, I'll bet that your sense of satisfaction dipped pretty low and that you weren't particularly motivated to prepare the report the next time it was due.

Figure 1

Managing People vs. Managing Work

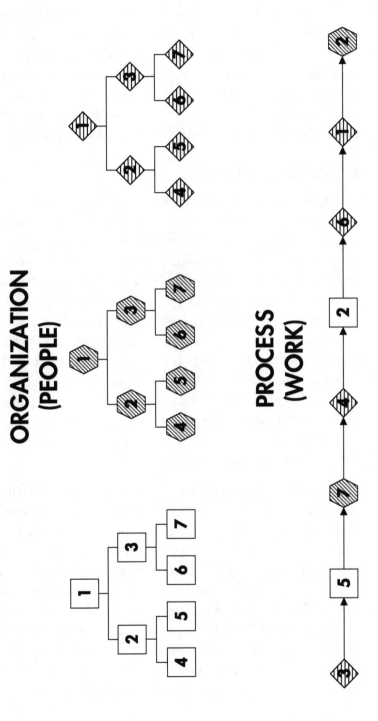

ORGANIZATION (PEOPLE)

PROCESS (WORK)

The message being sent was that your work was neither important nor valued by the organization. You may even have inferred that YOU were not valued by the organization. These situations are typical of people-depreciating conditions in organizations. Master Bosses are on the lookout for them, and once discovered, act quickly to fix them. By being alert to system dysfunction and gaps in ownership and then addressing them quickly, Master Bosses strongly communicate appreciation to their performers.

HR Policies and Practices

In most organizations, human resource policies serve primarily to punish the many for the sins of the few. Have you ever read an employee handbook that gave you the impression that if you signed on with that company you'd be working with a bunch of social outcasts or criminals? It probably listed all the infractions that could get you suspended without pay or terminated or perhaps even arrested. Most likely you'd never have thought of some of the antics that were mentioned. Such a document sends a negative, dis-empowering message about the workplace. The relationship it sets up between boss and performer is one of a critical parent trying to control a rebellious child. It doesn't leave much room for performer satisfaction, fulfillment and appreciation. Master Bosses are sensitive to the messages sent by their HR policies and practices. They take special care to ensure that HR policies and practices reflect the true values they want their organization to express.

A common and insidiously depreciating aspect of many companies' HR policies is their hierarchically based promotion structure. In virtually all of our client companies, the only route to financial advancement is promotion to supervisor or manager. This means that if I want to advance both financially and psychically, in terms of having a job with greater challenge and fulfillment potential, my only option is to move up hierarchically. This is a case of the company's **Ideal Target** not matching the employee's **Ideal Target**. This policy trap poses several dangers. First, I might not have the desire or inclination to become a supervisor, but I will take the promotion because I want to provide more for my family or improve my lifestyle. If you have ever worked for a boss who was really happier being a super salesperson, or an engineer, or a CNC machine operator, you know how painful that can be. Second, and far more important, I may not have the talent match to be a great boss. If I don't have the characteristics found within the company's **Ideal Target** for "Boss," then I shouldn't be considered for the position in the first place. The talent profile of a sales manager is far different than the talent profile of a super salesman. When we seduce someone whose talent profile doesn't match the requirements of the job into taking a hierarchical promotion, we hurt not only them but also the people who now report to them AND the departments that depend on their department for supply chain services. The results can and have laid companies low or even taken them down. General Motors, traditionally a product-driven company, suffered dearly in both financial performance and morale under the bean-counting mentality and values of accountant Roger Smith. I believe that this hierarchy trap is the root cause of the famous phenomenon known as the Peter Principle.[v]

So how do we aspirants to boss mastery avoid falling into this trap? The answer is simple but often overlooked. A client of mine in the retail distribution industry was struggling with a decline in profitability. In this product category, the volume of goods sold was the traditional measure of success. We began a transformation process in which sales reps and their managers would be compensated on a combination of territory volume AND profitability. The reps and managers initially resisted. They felt penalized if they happened to have a historically low profitability territory through no fault of their own. We solved the problem to everyone's satisfaction by ranking all 40-plus territories by profitability. We migrated the best-performing sales reps to the most profitable territories over a 12-month period, with an accompanying adjustment in base plus at-risk compensation. In this way, we created a scheme for matching sales rep performance with the amount of profit at risk in the territory they owned, while providing them an opportunity to increase their compensation without having to be promoted to sales manager.

With a little creative thought, most jobs can be infused with a scale of technical performance and compensated in a way that gives incumbents an incentive to perform at higher levels. This approach to building incentives at the non-supervisory level creates many more opportunities for performance-driven compensation than the ever shrinking funnel of higher levels of hierarchy.

Boss Behavior: The Ultimate Motivator

Abraham Maslow has taught us that people work for a variety of reasons. They may have a need for money to finance the basic necessities of life, a need for camaraderie with other human beings or a need for the satisfaction and meaning that comes from being a part of something worthy that is larger than they are.

The needs that motivate performers are revealed in the selection or promotion process that we have already described. The individual behavioral style foretells aspects of the work environment and the boss-performer relationship that the performer needs to feel comfortable and supported in achieving ambitious goals. The individual values provide clues to the kind of work and boss treatment that will stimulate the performer to do his best. The Master Boss continually embellishes this information by observing and listening to the performer. The Master Boss uses this information to guide her treatment of the performer so that he contributes his maximum discretionary effort.

Let's take a look at some guidelines the Master Boss uses, either consciously or unconsciously, to make interventions that support ownership while communicating care and respect. As mentioned earlier, human beings are stimulated to behave in ways that get their needs satisfied. Once I understand your needs, if I'm a Master Boss, I will adjust my behavior to align with, not oppose, your needs.

When a performer **earns** something that he **wants** by his behavior or performance, that outcome **positively reinforces** his behavior and he's motivated to practice more of that behavior. Positive reinforcement expands his behavior. When a performer **avoids** something that she **doesn't want**, like a reprimand or a salary cut, her behavior is **negatively reinforced**. Negative reinforcement limits her behavior. She simply avoids doing what she gets penalized for. When a performer **earns** something she **doesn't want**, the behavior that she was rewarded for is **extinguished**.

Consider this story of a client's painful experience with uninformed motivation. Mary was the top saleswoman at ABC Gadgets Inc. Not only did her customers contribute 40% of the total company revenue, they also accounted for 60% of ABC's repeat business. Bob, her boss and the owner of the company, was very appreciative of Mary's contribution and wanted to recognize her for it. He had a beautiful sterling silver plaque made and inscribed it with glowing words of praise. He then scheduled an all-hands meeting in the company auditorium and asked Mary to come to the podium. He spoke to the entire assembly in glowing terms about Mary's contributions and presented her with the plaque. To his astonishment, she began to sob and rushed out of the auditorium. The following day she submitted her resignation and went to work for a competitor.

Poor Bob. If he had only been paying attention he would have noticed that Mary's style was the exact opposite of the stereotypical super salesperson. She was very quiet and listened more than she spoke. She hated the glitzy PowerPoint presentation that the marketing department had created for introducing prospects to ABC's product line and used her own low-key version. She rarely got angry, except when someone tried to impose a deadline on her. Her customers raved about her problem-solving skills and her tenacity in helping them get at the cause of any gadget malfunction in their application. Mary was a very private, family-oriented person.

Bob's well-meaning gesture embarrassed her. Rather than feeling acknowledged, she was mortified by being publicly singled out and saw the plaque as a meaningless trinket. If Bob had been practicing some of the mastery behaviors we have been discussing, he would have used his knowledge of Mary's behavioral style and values to privately present her with a gift certificate for an all-expenses paid vacation for two on a secluded Caribbean Island. By rewarding Mary with something she didn't want, Bob extinguished her desire to be an ABC employee.

There are a host of other circumstances where boss behavior, thoughtfully considered and practiced, will make a performer feel appreciated and thereby be motivated to ever higher levels of discretionary effort. This is the essence of **Appreciation²** leadership.

THE COACH APPROACH: CREATING THE DISTINCTIONS OF PERFORMANCE MASTERY

The Master Boss, who uses Power of NO principles to inspire performers to accept the mantel of ownership for the work they do, is essentially functioning as a coach within the organization.

Coaches focus their attention on CONTEXT. They care about how performers see the game and how they relate to teammates and customers as the game unfolds. Coaches are less concerned with PROCESS (how the game is played) or CONTENT (the nitty-gritty of rules, boundaries, score-keeping, etc.).

If you or I are standing at home plate in Yankee Stadium, what do you think we see when Roger Clemens delivers a high hard one? I say that we're lucky to see anything at all. We might hear something that sounds like the psstt we hear when mosquito meets bug zapper on a warm summer evening. If we see anything, it's most likely a blur. For us, the context of this experience is probably fear of survival should this missile get too close and strike us before we can move to avoid it. Now let's switch scenarios. Instead of you or me at the plate, what if it were Barry Bonds or Mark McGwire? To them, that same Clemens fastball may look like a watermelon with "home run" written on it. The context of their experience might be something like: "Wow! It's right where I want it and it's outta here." Clearly, context is a complex condition of existence that is informed by a combination of skill, experience, talent, and point of view.

Coaches, using only their ability to speak and listen, can shift the performer's experience of the game – the context. In short, they can help performers move metaphorically from "survival threat" to "watermelon with home run written on it." When this happens, the performer's ability takes a quantum leap upward, never to return to the old baseline again.

The fundamental tool that coaches use to reframe the performer's context is the distinction. Officially, a distinction is defined as a linguistic abstraction that lives in experience. After that mouthful, it's clear that a concrete example will serve us far better. The distinction that anyone needs to ride a two-wheel bicycle is balance. Balance is just a word, a linguistic abstraction. But when you are hurtling down a gravel-covered hill at 30 miles per hour on your two-wheeler, it's much more than a word, isn't it? It lives in experience. That experience includes how you position your tush on the seat, the direction in which you turn the handlebar and the subtle way you lean to the left or the right. If you have low mastery of the distinction called balance, the context of hurtling down the hill on the two-wheeler is survival. You're thinking, "How do I keep from getting killed on this thing?" If your mastery of the distinction called balance is high, the context of the ride is: "Where can I go on this thing and how fast can I get there?"

The act of distinguishing is closely connected to the boundary-defining principles involved in the Power of NO. It's a way of articulating experience that transforms that experience for the performer. Remember the retail client that was suffering from declining profitability? His employees are inordinately proud of the superior service they provide to all their customers. Their service level is a matter of tradition and has contributed to their dominant competitive position in the markets they serve. When subjected to further scrutiny, this same source of pride is also a primary source of the firm's diminishing profitability. Pride in service leadership leads to their inability to say NO to unreasonable requests for special deliveries, or requests to build extra product inventory that is never consumed and must be disposed of at great expense when its shelf-life is exceeded. The company is failing to distinguish between service and servitude. The employees are afraid to say NO for fear of losing shelf space in their customer's stores. They are fearful of testing their belief that the quality of their products and services is so high that even if they lose space temporarily, the poor performance of their competition will drive their customer back to them and into a relationship of higher integrity and a greater spirit of win-win. As their coach, I continue to collaborate with them in finding low risk opportunities for substituting their fear-based assumptions with a more empowering reality.

SUMMARY

The path of Boss Mastery is not easy or comfortable, but it is the path to giving your performers a sense of ownership, and ultimately, it is the path to sustained enterprise profitability. Power of NO principles are part and parcel of the mastery journey. They help us match candidate talents with job requirements, generate and communicate clear job expectations and guide our behavior as stewards of the caring and respectful environment in which performers thrive. If we apply the Power of NO principles with discipline and consistency, our reward will be an employee population that feels appreciated and in turn appreciates. By concentrating on producing the condition I've described as **Appreciation^2**, you will have a business that performs beyond your wildest imaginings. I hope you embark on the journey today. Good luck!

*   *   *   *   *   *   *

i   Buckingham, Marcus and Curt Coffman, *First Break All the Rules: What the World's Greatest Managers Do Differently*, (Simon & Schuster, May 1999).

ii   The DISC model is based on the work of William Moulton Marston. For more details, see "DISC: The Universal Language," a reference manual by Bill J. Bonnstetter, Judy I. Suiter, & Randy Widrick published by Target Training International, Ltd.

iii Hunter, John E. & Ronda F. Hunter, "Validity and Utility of Alternative Predictors of Job Performance," <u>Psychological Bulletin</u>, Vol. 96, No. 1. 1984, p 90.

iv   Deming, W. Edwards, *Out of the Crisis*, (MIT Press, 1986).

v   Peter, Laurence J. and Raymond Hull, *The Peter Principle*, (Buccaneer Books, October 1996).

ABOUT HANK EPSTEIN

After serving a Fortune 100 corporation for 25 years in management positions in technology, manufacturing, planning and marketing, including a stint as the leader of a pilot re-engineering effort for a $4 billion unit of that corporation, **Hank Epstein** created The Quality Coach® in 1991.

Together with his life and business partner, Jeanne Gladden, Hank is living his deep commitment to help people connect personal fulfillment with business success. He believes that the 21st century will offer unlimited possibilities for individuals to derive fulfillment from their work. However, they must learn to let go of their traditional expectations for security in and constancy of the workplace. They must embrace change and, whether self-employed or not, become 100% response-able for adding value to their customers, delivering services at the lowest possible cost and continuously improving work processes.

Hank is a certified Situational Leadership© and Coaching Clinic© instructor, a certified Theory of Constraints consultant and is affiliated with Coach University. He is a member of the International Coaches Federation.

CHAPTER VII.

The Forensics of Financial Decision Making: The Good, the Bad, and the Ugly

Margaret DeMotte

They told you that all customers were worth your effort; that all customers are the same; that they all benefit your company. I'm here to tell you, they are wrong! Not all customers add the same amount to your bottom line. Some may even cost you money. Should you give that deeper discount because you need the business? Does it make sense to increase your loss on certain business for volume? You'll just increase your losses. If your mind is made up that all customers are alike and are beneficial to your company, you may want to skip this chapter. On the other hand, you may want to read further, just to verify how right you are.

If you have gotten this far, you surely see how the Positive Power of NO can give you a strategic edge. You understand the benefit of determining an organizational philosophy and direction. When you set limits, employees know what is expected of them. You are in the business of helping them appreciate. The whole organization understands the direction the company wants to go and is ready to let go of unproductive tasks and ways of thinking. You know what you don't want to be and what you will not do. The Positive Power of NO resides within you and your organization.

NOT ALL CUSTOMERS (OR PRODUCTS, OR INDUSTRIES) ARE CREATED EQUAL!

The stage is set for you to take your organization in a new direction. You now have to decide what that direction will be. It is my job to show you how to identify what makes some customers not so great. Then maybe you can avoid giving away the farm to those or new clients. You can concentrate on the customers, products or industries that accelerate your business along your strategic path. This chapter will help you determine the right business mix.

It was late at night and, as usual, there was a light on in only one office. Wearily, Ralph shook his head. He just didn't understand. For the past couple of years, the profits from his small manufacturing firm had been lackluster. Yet not much had changed. Yes, competition was heating up, but he wasn't losing customers. Last year Ralph knew he had to do something. Increasing sales had always fixed it before, so he brought all the sales people together and declared, "We need more sales!" And the sales force did just what was asked.

A year later, Ralph was poring over the year-end results, and they weren't good. In fact they were worse than last year. Yes, sales were up. "But where did the profits go?" Ralph thought. The dark closed in on him and he shut his eyes.

In the light of the next morning, the employees bustled as Ralph made his way to his office. It was still disheveled from the night before. The sinking feeling in the pit of his stomach was still there. Ralph reached for the phone and dialed the CFO's extension. "Jim, can you come in here?" When Jim appeared at the door, all Ralph could muster was "What happened?" As Jim droned on about percentages, ratios and trends, all his words blended together. It didn't make sense. "OK," said Ralph. "But what *really* happened?"

"We sold too much to the *wrong* customers," Jim stated flatly and without emotion.

"What do you mean 'WRONG'?" Ralph blurted, with a lot more emotion than Jim.

"I mean that most of the new sales brought in last year were at a lot lower margin than our regular business." Jim waited for a response, but when none came, he went on. "You see, we were under orders to increase sales. Our sales force had to lower the prices, give bigger discounts. Some new customers haven't paid in over 60 days. And others had special requests that manufacturing could not satisfy without a great deal of trouble. Remember that six-figure job we did last November? After commissions and all the reruns we had to do, not to mention the expenses associated with proposals and all of the wining and dining, we barely broke even."

While Ralph still did not respond, the look on his face told the CFO that he was starting to understand. Ralph never knew what hit him.

Are you like Ralph? Do you know which business makes you the most money? Which customers are easiest to work with? Which orders are easiest to produce? Which ones meet the requirements of your strategic plan? Even if you are producing a homogeneous product or service, your customers are not homogeneous. How do you identify those customers or products that don't help you toward your goal?

You probably already have a system that can tell you what business is profitable, which customers pay their invoices on time and which orders move fastest through the plant. I'm not going to tell you to change your system or tell you how to create one. There will be no list of "musts," no one-size-fit-all profile of the perfect customer. You will have to determine what characteristics you need in a customer or product. I will merely walk you through some checkpoints in the process of determining those traits. No one will tell you to get rid of some clients or products on your way to your strategic goals. These decisions are entirely yours. What's important is making that decision through thoughtful analysis. Decisions made in the heat of the moment are likely to be different from one day to the next. They will depend on the customer, on who brought the problem to your attention or even on your mood. Strategic planning is put to work through information and numbers. They make strategic issues real. Decide what direction your company should go and then determine which industries, customers and products that support that vision. There will always be some that are more supportive than others.

When Ralph accepted whatever business came through his door, he was surprised by the results. Some years were good and others not so good. Only when he had several not-so-good years in succession did he decide to act. After thoughtful consideration, Ralph's firm determined that it could *not* focus only on making customers happy. It had to focus on making the *right* customers happy. This change was not easy for the organization, but think of the stress Ralph no longer has to deal with. Everyone in his firm now knows who is a fit and who isn't. The business that no longer fits the profile will not be "kicked upstairs" for decisions on concessions. Instead Customer Service is allowed to deal with it appropriately, by saying "NO."

Do you remember Susan Bishop from Chapter 4? When she took whatever business that came through her door, Bishop Partners found it difficult to remain in business. And they had "good" clients, clients who paid them six figures for one contract. But perhaps, too, they found out that the large contracts are not necessarily the most profitable. After thoughtful consideration Bishop Partners determined that they could *not* focus on only making customers happy but they had to focus on making the *right* customers happy. They could identify the *right* client when he came through the door by matching the client with six characteristics (specific industry, appropriate rank of executive searched for, high probability of repeat business, desirous of a consultative partnership, realistic about pay scales for new hires, and companies considered "Employers of choice" with no bad press or reputation). Now this change was not easy for the organization, nor for Bishop personally. But in the end she had not only the clients she preferred, but also a profitable enterprise.[i]

Bishop Partners changed in other ways as well. For example, their staffing and HR policies had to change to support the new direction. You have read in previous chapters how setting limits or boundaries can help your firm and you individually in meeting choices, changes, policy, and people issues. While I will be dealing with determining the right business mix, you might find some of these steps valuable in other areas as well.

You may understand what business you don't want simply by being in business and "seeing it all." The division between business you want and business you don't want may be crystal clear. If so, you may want to jump to the next chapter and apply what you know. However, there may still be value in reviewing these steps. Things change – markets, product costs, new innovations, etc. And maybe, just maybe, things aren't really what they seem. Remember, Ralph's firm had difficult customers not only in profitability but also credit and manufacturing. What seems obvious to you may not be obvious to your staff. The give and take in discussing the limits will define, stretch and redefine those limits, and that process will improve both the organization and the people in it. Determining which clients you don't want is just as important, if not more so, than determining what clients you do want. So where do we begin? As I go through the possible steps I will be referring to "customers." However, depending on your business or strategy, you can substitute "product" or "industry." Using an **Anything Goes Target** (see inside front cover) for any of these will negatively impact your profits. Regardless, your organization probably has all the information you need. Gather your staff together. If a section of the organization is not represented, invite someone from that department. They just might have that bit of knowledge you need.

EVALUATION OF THE "NOT-SO-GREAT" CUSTOMER

Ralph and Jim started to make a list of all the problems that occurred during the year. As the list grew, they called several managers for clarifications. To Ralph's surprise, each one gave them more issues to put on the list. Each problem pointed to issues with a customer or sale – warning flags on credit reports, requests for deeper discounts, 10 sales calls or more, requests for product modifications, proposal after expensive proposal. As Ralph and Jim picked at the list, they started another one. This list contained the qualities of the customer that made sense for their business.

That list had the qualities of their "good" customers. On the other, they listed qualities of their "not-so-good customers." "Good" is defined differently by different areas of the company. Jim looks at profitability. Credit looks at payment history, Customer Service sees the "hassle factor," while Production knows which customers cause the greatest chaos in the plant. Each department's point of view is valid and none is more important than the others. Every department contributes to the relationship between Ralph and his customers. Likewise, any department can make or break your business.

Through this process, Ralph discovered that you define what you want in a customer by what you don't want. Ralph found that one-time contracts, while fine for that moment, did not offer his company any long-term success. He now requires new clients to present opportunities for repeat business. In order to determine whether a client presents such opportunities, Ralph Inc. would have to ask the client a question such as, "How many placement contracts do you let each year?" Saying you don't want customers that pay slowly may not help you identify such a potential client, and the definition of "slow pay" may vary from one day to the next. But take a stab at the definition by examining your own clients' pay history for help. At the end of the list making, if the bullet points are fuzzy, work to sharpen them up. In other words, start defining those limits, sharpen the line between red and yellow, move toward the **Ideal Target**.

1ˢᵀ CHECKPOINT –
ARE ALL AREAS OF THE BUSINESS REPRESENTED IN THE CHARACTERISTICS?

Identify all departments that are the roots of the issues. Those departments should have the information, reports or numbers that you'll need to define your limits. Many times you are already capturing the information you need. Other times you may find it necessary to start a process to gather that information. It is important to engage in a dialog that explores all aspects of the "Good" and "Not-So-Good" lists. Is there an area that is not represented? Where else can information be found? Is there any overlap or underlap in your lists?

As Jim and Ralph developed the "Good" and "Not-So-Good" lists, they found that one area led them to another. Manufacturing talked about customers whose demands for improved delivery caused rework issues. Now Jim captured rework costs in the manufacturing analysis. But they still weren't capturing the safety issues that Manufacturing brought up.

"Do we keep records like that?" Ralph asked. The Manufacturing manager sure didn't. "They handle all the Workers' Comp claims in HR, but they are not identified by job," she explained. After a quick revision by the HR manager and Manufacturing manager, the larger incidents were identified by job. The results had an impact on how Ralph and Jim viewed the ranking of their customers. It didn't take long for HR and Manufacturing to develop a feedback loop to Jim for inclusion in job costing. HR and Manufacturing were not involved in other aspects of the list making. But they were now eager to share their opinions as to what should be on those lists.

QUALITIES IN LIMITS

After much discussion, the qualities of the "Good" customers emerged for Ralph's team. While profits were primary, other issues were factored in. During the discussions, the sales manager said, "So I guess I should only be looking for customers who fit this profile!" "Well," asked Jim, "when would you like to know that a customer falls below the "Good" line into the "Ugly" or the "Bad" category, Ralph?" Ralph looked over his glasses and said only one word: "Now!"

"I can't go out and just find customers in the "Good" category. What am I going to ask? 'Are you going to be a profitable customer for us?'" stammered the sales manager.

The HR manager spoke up, "When I interview potential employees, I can ask certain questions that reveal when a prospect will be either a hard worker or someone who is looking for an easy time. Why can't we take the qualities in our "Good" customers and develop questions for Jim to ask that will tell us what type of customer they might be." The nods in agreement were all Ralph needed to proceed.

Ralph's management team eventually developed five qualities that made sense for their business. You'll notice that each quality can be put in the form of a question to be asked during the sales process.

- No fewer than 6 orders placed in a year

- Not less than $100,000 in yearly orders

- No structural product line modifications

- Will not be considered "second source"

- Will not ask for terms outside 2 / 10 net 30

While Ralph didn't define them as such, his team set limits. Limits will also help you measure the progress of your organization toward your goals. Ralph's team determined that customers who can't generate $100,000 in sales are not the most profitable. Since situations change, however, if the profitability of these customers increases, then the cut-off limit could be dropped to say, $85,000. Wouldn't they want to monitor that relationship? If the profitability of these customers remains the same, then it is steady as she goes. If it doesn't, corrections to the limit should be made, but only with forethought and consideration.

So, how does Ralph determine which limits to use? Are there "no-brainers" that are easily identified and easily measured and speak to the new direction of the company? Those go on the top of the list. But you also may need to define more complicated rules. If you determine that you don't want customers with orders under $100,000, you may find that you also don't want companies that pay over 60 days, or companies that demand lower quality specs, or even orders over $5 million, etc. Business is never one-dimensional. To decide on the secondary limits, ask the questions: Can I identify customers that have those qualifications? Can I track the results of customers I have with qualifications I don't want and those with qualifications I do? How do both groups affect my business outcomes and my progress toward my long-term goals? Does this limit significantly affect my business or my profitability? You can rank your lists based on the answers to these or similar questions.

There is one final test for limits: Can it be clearly defined in terms that everyone in the organization can understand and agree upon? "Bills not paid within 60 days" is better than "slow pay." The limits must be defined in terms of characteristics of a customer. If "profitability" is to be a limit, what characteristic in the customer relates to profit? Sales level? Product line? Returned goods? You can't ask a prospect if they intend to be profitable. And you can't wait until the sale is completed and the books closed to see if they are. You have to use your historical information to identify the relationship between profitability and sales volume or defective returns. Ralph Inc. identified relationships (6 orders a year totaling over $100,000) that determined profitability. The sales team needs to be able to translate limits into questions.

2ND CHECKPOINT –
ARE LIMITS CONSISTENT WITH CORPORATE GOALS?

The limits you set should be compatible with your corporate mission. If they're not, your employees will not know what to do when a conflict arises and they will bring all such problems to you to resolve. Or the limits will be followed and your company will end up facing a different direction than where your strategic initiative was aimed. Or you will be headed in the expected direction but you will be going broke. If there are major issues, you may want to re-evaluate your strategic direction.

Ralph was still feeling uneasy. What about opening that new market? It might be years before customers in that new market will produce yearly orders over $100,000. Yet less than a year ago the team had decided to go after this new market. How can they now justify moving into that market knowing that it will not produce immediate results?

"We made that decision after much debate and analysis," said Jim.

"Yet we can't have potential customers from that market rejected because they are outside our limits. And our traditional market may change as customers' needs change or when our competitors start undercutting," countered Ralph.

The management team decided to re-evaluate their two decisions to determine how compatible they were. The concern was to produce a direction for the company that could be understood and followed by all employees. They decided that the limits must speak to that new direction. If the entire company was moving from a market with which it has experience and results to one with which it has little, it had better understand both the opportunities and the risks. But this made the determination of limits more difficult. Certain assumptions had to be made to define and quantify those limits. During the discussions, Ralph's team raised several questions. "Will customers ordering 50,000 units a year really make us profitable?" "Are there enough of those customers in the market who will meet our criteria?" "How will we know if it's working?"

The managers decided to update the reporting system to create a constant monitoring of the numbers. This would make the strategic planning real. Ralph wanted to be sure that he had systems in place to provide good feedback. "We will need to review the results and discuss what can be changed to improve the situation. Since we agree that this new market is important to the continued success of our company, we need to determine the goals and limits for this segment of our business. However, if we find that this market does not have the potential to meet the limits for the rest of our business, we will drop that market. Now, let's decide what the limits will be for this new market and how long we will give it to produce."

HIDE AND SEEK, OR WHERE ARE THE LIMITS?

So Ralph's team defined the limits that support their strategic issues. They were clearly communicated to the employees who would apply them. But team members still struggled with setting an exact number for sales. They knew that sales volume was critical but weren't sure of the number.

In defining limits, you sometimes need to look past the obvious. "Difficult" customers may lead you to a product that has quality-control problems. Thus the disqualification (the opposite of qualification) of such customers will not be on their demands for customer service but on their quality specifications or the product line they buy. If that customer were purchasing another product line, would you still consider him "difficult?" If you don't trace the issue back to its source, you may be asking the wrong questions and disqualifying potentially profitable customers.

It took more than one department in Ralph's company to supply the information needed to set precise limits. It was easy to determine that customers who place more than 6 orders and buy more than $100,000 a year are profitable. Jim found that information in the sales and cost reports produced each month by the MIS department. But the last three limits were not routinely analyzed. It took several days of discussion and analysis by the entire management team. Jim brought up the cost of customers paying beyond terms. But it took input from Manufacturing and Customer Service to figure out how product line modifications and their vendor ranking affected profitability. The information wasn't readily available; it had to be constructed out of reports only available in the Manufacturing and Customer Service areas. Ralph charged the managers of these departments to formalize their reports. In fact, the management team wanted all of the statistics that kept track of the five limits reported at the monthly management meeting. Ralph knew from experience that he could not just set the limits and forget about them. He remembered setting other procedures in place and then stepping aside. The result was a slow but steady death of the procedure.

You can't gather the information only once, set the limits and go merrily on your way. You must be able to review the results as a part of your management process. Limit-oriented thinking must be internalized, much as you need to internalize the Positive Power of NO within yourself. It must become part of your culture. Make your information system accommodate perpetual limit information and result-gathering.

3ʳᵈ Checkpoint – Can limits be quantified in relationship to corporate goals?

From Checkpoint #2 you have determined that your limits are compatible with your strategic directions. The prospects who fail to disqualify themselves are the ones that you feel will help support your strategic goal of better profitability. Still, there are two errors you can make: failing to disqualify the wrong prospect, and disqualifying the right prospect. Make sure your reporting system is telling you that sales volume actually does equal better profitability, and that a customer with $100,000 in annual sales will provide the desired level of profitability (because they do now and have in the past).

HOW DO YOUR CUSTOMERS MATCH UP?

Jim had a great handle on his reporting system for sales, cost and profitability. So he decided to use the five limits to rank Ralph Inc.'s current customers. If it worked on the customers for whom he had history, it should work on prospects. Jim was looking for problems in applying the limits to the customers. When he asked Customer Service or Manufacturing a question about an existing customer, did they understand what he was asking? Were their answers consistent with purpose of the limit?

Next to each customer's name, Jim put the number of orders placed each year from the sales database. Then he listed the total sales for the last 12 months. Product line modifications were a little harder to determine, since the reporting system for that limit had just been created. But Engineering came to the rescue by opening up its computer records to Jim. The column for this limit was a simple "Yes" or "No." The next column, labeled "Second Source," also required a yes-or-no answer. If Ralph Inc. had been getting orders only when another (preferred) supplier could not fulfill the request, Jim entered a "Yes" in this column. But it was the limit on terms that gave him problems. You see, the limit started out as "Will not ask for terms outside net 30." When Jim added the customer terms and then sorted the list by profitability, he noticed that some of the better customers did not have just net 30. If the limit was not at net 30, where should it be?

Jim's results for his set of strategic limits were similar to the findings of Vilfredo Pareto. The Italian economist, at the turn of the previous century, observed that 20% of the Italian population owned 80% of the accumulated wealth. He termed this phenomenon the "Vital Few and Trivial Many Rule." Today we call it the 80/20 rule. This mix of 80%-20% reminds us that equal effort does not yield equal results. This rule of thumb applies when measuring effectiveness against diminishing returns on resources (such as money and time). More than likely there will be a natural break in your current customer ranking. It may not be 80/20. It may be 70/30 or 50/50. But there will be a break. Use these natural breaks to sharpen the limit between the bull's-eye and the red ring on your **Ideal Target**.

4ᵗʰ Checkpoint –
When applied to the customer base,
do limits produce strong dividing lines?

As the team debated what terms would not be acceptable, Ralph asked, "Who cares about a dividing line? Can't you just pick a place that you like? What difference does it make?"

You are practicing on your current customer base. If it does not produce clear results, neither will the limits when applied to new business. Remember we are looking for that **Ideal Target**. You may have eliminated the **Anything Goes** and the **Big Fuzzy Targets**, but an unclear dividing line will only lead to a smaller **Better Fuzzy Target**, where the boundaries between red and yellow are still unclear. A sharp dividing line ensures not only that the limits are appropriate but also that they are executable and can produce results.

"A crisp dividing line makes sure that the limits can be communicated to Marketing or Sales for their use." Jim answered. "You see, Sales and Marketing will be making commitments to your clients and prospects. If they don't understand the limits, they can be making promises that we can't afford or don't want to keep. They need to know the limits and how to apply them when making commitments to our customers. If the division is not sharp, they may feel there is room for negotiation or they can talk you into it because it is not clear if this is business you want. Those in direct contact with our customers must understand that the limits are clear and precise. And management must understand that adhering to those limits will produce the customer that falls in the upper portion of our business."

So what happens if there is no strong dividing line? Three areas need to be reviewed for their accuracy – the *relationship* between the stated limit and the desired result, the *reporting system* for current business and the *weighting* of the limits to make sure the most important limit has the most effect on the list. Adjust where necessary and try again. In extreme circumstances, you may need to go back and re-evaluate all the qualities of the "Good" and "Not-So-Good" customers. By leaving out a limit or adding one, the division line may become more distinct.

recently, cab drivers in Washington, D.C., refused to pick up African-American passengers. They said the risk of robbery was too great. The public outcry forced them to reverse this discriminatory, unethical and possibly illegal practice.

While you may not be faced with such legal or ethical problems when determining your limits, you may still be faced with prejudices or preferences. A salesperson may prefer calling on customers in Florida and not the frozen North. A customer may have been a favorite of the sales manager who just left. Input from certain departments is ignored based on the how much the manager is disliked. Just be aware of human frailties and try to set the limits based on legitimate business reasons.

THE RIGHT MIX – THE RIGHT RESULT

Isn't that what you're after? What makes sense for your company? What are your core values? Your strategic plan? What must customers/products look like to put you on the path to better results?

Limits will defend your plan in the everyday battle to win profitable business. By focusing sales resources on prospects who exhibit qualities of the upper 20%, you'll move your results there too. You must be clear in your limits, committed to the disqualification of prospects and have the courage not to "adjust" the limits under pressure. It will not be easy.

Or you can hope the next big order is profitable. You can guess what the results will be. You can plan all you want, but what happens after that? I hear that Ralph has a lamp for sale. You know, the one in which he burned the midnight oil! He won't be needing it any more.

*　*　*　*　*　*　*

i　Bishop, Susan. "The Strategic Power of Saying No," Harvard Business Review, Nov./Dec. 1999, pp 4-11.

ABOUT MARGARET DeMOTTE

Margaret became aware that all customers are not created equal in her very first position. While working for a "job shop," it became obvious that differences in financials from month to month were not due just to coincidence. Thirty years of manufacturing accounting has given Margaret a unique window into the implications of manufacturing and selling any product or service to any customer. By identifying products or customers that do not improve the bottom line, she has helped her firms not only improve sales, but also profitability.

Margaret is an accounting sleuth, ferreting out causes of the impediments to profitability. She specializes in inventory control (cutting inventories as much as 20% per year), and costing (exposing the true contribution of products, customers, and industries to the bottom line). Margaret has developed automated systems for cost analysis and has worked heavily with manufacturing, costing, and sales departments to implement product tracking systems.

Margaret has a BA in Economics and Business Administration and an MBA with an emphasis on Finance from Webster University in St. Louis, Missouri.

CONGRATULATIONS BENSON...
ONCE AGAIN YOU HAVE US
COMPETING IN THE WRONG ARENA.

CHAPTER VIII.

Brilliance Marketing:
It's all about *subtracting* from the equation everything at which you are less than brilliant until you are left with a tight and piercing beam of light

Celia Rocks

A lighthouse is powerful because it focuses its energy into a beam that clearly illuminates all that is safe – and every area of danger, too. That's why I use the lighthouse as a symbol for "Brilliance Marketing." When you get rid of fuzzy, scattered, shaky and anything else that's not focused, what remains will be your *brilliance* – simply put, what you and your people do best!

It's all about *subtracting* from the equation everything at which you are less than brilliant until you are left with a tight, piercing beam of light. Customers who are wrong for you will eliminate themselves by ignoring your beam. Those who are right for you will be drawn to it like ships that know they have found their way to safe harbor.

The first step is the hardest. I find that companies, and individuals, often have trouble identifying their brilliance. Sometimes they are so busy saying "Yes" to things they are not particularly good at that their best talents or services get edged out of the limelight. These are people, clearly, who have not learned the Power of No.

The **Anything Goes Target** will not do. If you try to persuade prospects that you are good at everything, they may conclude that you are brilliant in nothing. You don't need to have an answer to every buyer's problem. However, you must be notably good at satisfying at least one need, and the key feature of your product or service must stand out.

Your special brilliance does not have to be earth-shaking or even unique. But it does have to *matter*, to be *real* and *important* to both the company and its customers.

Examples? As I write this section I am drinking a sixteen-ounce bottle of water because it is refreshing, convenient, and good for me. I chose this bottle over its competitors because it comes in a size I can slip into my purse and it fits the cup holder in my car. So the brilliance in this bottle of water is in its convenient size.

I have a friend who shops for clothing almost exclusively at Chico's, a chain of high-end boutiques in fashionable shopping centers around the country. Along with designing clothes that offer a little more coverage over the hips or a little more wiggle room around the waist, Chico's developed its own sizing method. Chico's dresses are sized 0, 1, 2 or 3. My friend, who is a normal size 12 to 14, can walk into a fashion-friendly environment and pick a size 2 or 3 off the rack. No more rifling through the segregated "women's" sizes in the department store. No more encountering a size 6 outfit you like, only to learn that the designer has not chosen to share his exquisite ensemble with the size-14 crowd. Chico's showcases its brilliance through its innovative sizing.

The Bernstein Law Firm, P.C., a Pittsburgh law office that I have worked with on marketing, has three marvelous strengths, all beginning with the letter "T." That allowed us to use alliteration as an underline below the firm's name: Tradition + Technology + Talent. The firm had a proven *tradition* of providing excellent service over its thirty-five years in business. It had the *technology* – an electronic interface with the courts – to serve its clients better. Finally, the firm had consistently hired and kept the best and brightest *talent* in its specialty of creditors' rights.

I typically ask a client to complete three sentences:

1. **I am happiest at work when...**
2. **What sets us apart from the competition is that we offer...**
3. **We are able to do this because...**

Here is how the manager of a trucking firm completed those sentences:

1. **I am happiest at work when** *I am able to meet or exceed my customer's expectations.*
2. **What sets us apart from the competition is that we offer** *unsurpassed service and maintain an exemplary safety record.*
3. **We are able to do this because** *we hire the most qualified truck drivers and offer them state-of-the-art advanced driver training and safety instruction.*

When you have a string of "ands" in your description of brilliance, you probably haven't zeroed in enough. You cannot be all things to all people. And trying to do so is the best way I know to compromise your true brilliance.

Genuine brilliance gives energy and direction to your business, whereas unfocused action drains you of energy and makes you a victim of a **Fuzzy Target**.

A BANK DEAL THAT WORKED FOR BOTH SIDES

On December 1, 2001, Mellon Financial Corporation announced the sale of its mid-Atlantic retail and small business banking operations to Citizens Financial Group for $2.1 billion. This was a rare deal because it allowed both parties to focus on their brilliance, and both to expand their operations.

Mellon and Citizens Financial had been moving in entirely different directions. In the previous few years, Mellon had discovered that it was truly brilliant at providing fee-based services, such as asset management and processing, to wealthy individuals and corporations. At the same time, Mellon had essentially been ignoring its retail banking operations, which served people of more modest wealth.

Along came Citizens Financial Group. Its brilliance was retail banking. It offered outstanding customer services to clients of average means. More importantly, unlike Mellon, it *wanted* to expand the retail side.

The deal has been a success so far. Mellon invested the money it received from the sale of the retail outlets into its area of brilliance, which is fee-based businesses. As a result, Mellon strengthened its hold on the number one position in trust fees among U.S. banks.

Citizens, meanwhile, has been a hit with both clients and employees across Pennsylvania. Not only has it managed to please retail customers with a slew of new services, it has also retained all of Mellon's employees and kept all of Mellon's former branches open.

Each bank said "No" to something that it was not doing particularly well and that it judged the other bank could do better. By eliminating services in which it was sub-par, Mellon freed energy and resources to concentrate on an area where it was doing stellar work.

Perhaps most remarkable of all is that the two companies have continued to cooperate after the sale. Citizens chose Mellon to manage significant components of its employee-retirement plan and has been selling Mellon's Dreyfus mutual funds at all of its bank branches.

THE NEED TO SAY "NO" TO NON-BRILLIANT COMMUNICATIONS

To be a Brilliance Marketer you have to be **ruthless** in your rejection of well-intentioned efforts that fail to communicate your brilliance effectively. Good intentions are not enough. They may produce "nice" marketing pieces and programs, maybe even ones that really appeal to people. But those pieces and programs fall short of your best, and you should say "No!" to them.

Weed out everything that doesn't trumpet your brilliance.

A bank where I'd had some accounts publishes a newsletter. One recent issue featured drawings of sailboats on the front. I liked the drawings but I wasn't sure what I was supposed to conclude. Did my bank favor customers who enjoyed sailing? It wasn't clear.

Another newsletter came from a local printer. This letter was full of canned features, games, horoscopes, etc., none of which had anything to do with promoting quality printing. Now, what this particular printer is good at is offering customers a wide selection of printing papers, in many colors, textures, and weights. To highlight their brilliance they could have sent out a book of samples to customers, instead of the goofy, irrelevant newsletter. I would have been happy to keep the sample book close at hand to match paper with projects as we were making our printing decisions. Their newsletter, however, I tossed in the wastebasket.

BE WARY OF HIGHLIGHTING YOUR WEAK SPOTS!

Sometimes when the captain of a ship lost at sea thinks he sees a rescuing beam from a lighthouse, he really is catching a glimpse of the cold, merciless moon. Similarly, beware! What looks like a dramatic highlight may be something you should fix, not feature.

Sheraton Hotels, owned by Starwood Hotels & Resorts Worldwide, realized in 2002 that it had an image problem. "The brand continues to be known in North America for lousy customer service and shabby digs," executives said (as quoted in *The Wall Street Journal,* Sept. 6, 2002, p. B1).

So what did Sheraton decide to do to help fill its empty rooms?

The company decided to focus its marketing on a customer-service quality guarantee. Guests who were not happy with their rooms or their staff interactions would be given cash for their bad experience! No bath mat? An easy $20 off the room price. Slow room service? You won't have to pay full price for your meal!

This scheme had a fatal flaw: These messages highlighted Sheraton's weaknesses. It's as if they said, "We know we're performing badly, but we want to reward you for putting up with our inadequacies and the inconveniences you're bound to suffer when you stay with us."

The money-back-for-bad-service guarantee did nothing but lather gold leaf and spit on top of a festering wound. It illuminated the very thing Sheraton was having the most trouble with.

A Brilliance Marketing approach would zero in on positive features that Sheraton could highlight in its advertising and public relations appeals to the public. Since its properties are older and its service has sometimes been sub-par, Sheraton should look for other things to build on. Most Sheratons are conveniently located, clean, and good value for the money. These are items far more worthy of highlighting than missing bath mats and slow room service!

WHAT THAT NEEDS ATTENTION ARE YOU NOT MANAGING

Even in relatively small businesses the left hand rarely knows what the right hand is doing. Count the number of hands in your business and you'll get an idea of how complex and challenging it is to coordinate the actions of all. Most of the time we don't really know whether what we or our associates are doing is consistent with what we believe our special brilliance to be.

Most firms touch their customers, employees, distributors, and other important constituencies in an amazing hodgepodge of ways. At any given time there may be a new product launch, a sales program or some other centrally coordinated effort going on. But all these efforts combined will probably affect no more than 10% to 20% of what is visible to the company's customers.

The more routine things going on simultaneously are not factored into the big picture and are, essentially, unmanaged. At least we can say they are unmanaged as they affect customer relations or satisfaction.

The questions are these: How many ways do we communicate every day in business, and are we managing those communications to assure that they project an **Ideal Target** and reflect our brilliance?

Not long ago my firm was invited to make a Brilliance Marketing Management presentation to a leading management-consulting group in the Northeast. The firm's main source of revenue derived from working with companies in trouble and turning them around.

An associate and I arrived at the management consultant's office promptly at 9 a.m. on a Tuesday. As we exited the elevator across from the entrance to their office, we noticed that the front door was propped open by what looked like a large stick. On closer look I could see that this pitiful stick was a Ficus tree on its last leg. A few withered leaves clung to its stark branches.

"How can these people expect to breathe life into failing companies when they can't even breathe life into a tree at their own door?" I remarked to my associate.

The firm's dead Ficus tree practically screamed, "Inattention! Neglect! Uncaringness!" "Failure!"

We immediately recommended that before the firm looked at any sophisticated systems for soliciting new customers or better ways to achieve turnarounds, they replace the dead Ficus tree and commit to keeping the new one in good health. They agreed to do so and we moved on to other issues.

Now let me give you an example of a firm that showcases its brilliant customer relations strength in even the most casual encounters. This is a computer-solutions firm called Strategic Technologies Inc., known to employees and customers as STI.

Founder and former Washington Redskins cornerback Mike Shook likes to say, "We bear hug the customer with value."

A friend of mine was impressed out of his socks when he walked into the front lobby on an occasion when the receptionist had, momentarily, been called away from her station. He had not been waiting long when an employee happened through the lobby and immediately issued a warm greeting, inquired whom the visitor wished to see, and offered to get him coffee, tea, or a soft drink.

When the visitor remarked to Shook about this red-carpet treatment from an employee who had nothing to do with providing reception-area duties, he was told, "Any one of our people would have done the same for you."

In other words, STI had developed a culture in which warm outreach to visitors, customers, or anyone else who came through the door was second nature. That is a good example of "living your brilliance."

SOME FINAL WORDS OF TOUGH ADVICE

Let's face it head-on: Business these days often amounts to war. And marketing is a viciously competitive battlefield. The marketplace, in most fields, has five to ten times as many competitors as it had a decade ago. And many of these competitors are well-established bruisers with huge battle chests.

To win in the marketplace, you have to stand out as different – and better – than your competitors in some significant areas. It's not enough to be acceptable in quantity, quality, price, service, follow-through, etc. You need to be absolutely MEMORABLE in at least one respect.

Be careful to avoid diluting your efforts. Many marketers, we find, do "a little of this and a little of that." Their marketing program becomes a laundry list of activities. But laundry lists do not make good marketing plans! The best approach is to *say "no" to the mediocre, find the winning actions and focus all your strength behind those.*

Do you really want to talk to everyone who reads your ads? Probably not. Your most productive use of time will be to dialog with qualified prospects who understand that you have something to offer that meets a very specific need of theirs. Talking at any length with other inquirers will no doubt prove a waste of time.

I also recommend concentrating your marketing efforts into *powerful bursts.* Spreading out your campaign over too long a period may dilute its effects. A six- to-eight-week campaign may work better than one that lasts half a year.

What's more, you must understand and respect your limitations. I've seen marketers who try to compete for attention in arenas where they do not have enough power to succeed. Television ads are an example. When a mid-sized or regional competitor uses prime-time television to court customers, its commercials may pale in comparison to those aired by national advertisers. The smaller advertiser inadvertently portrays itself as weak and ineffectual by comparison.

Competing in the *wrong arena* is a surefire way to accentuate your weaknesses instead of highlighting your strengths. It is better to be the most impressive commercial on late-night cable than the least impressive ad on local prime-time network television.

Finally, don't force things. Refrain from being so aggressive that you, in effect, are forcing yourself or your products upon customers.

Plato wrote (in *The Republic*), "*Each citizen should play his part in the community according to his individual gifts.*" When you are forcing it, you are stepping beyond that natural part in the community and trying to push yourself in ways that do not fit. Brilliance Marketing steps back and takes a good hard look at what your firm's individual gifts are…and are not…and then finds natural, even easy, ways to build relationships and reap sales based on those gifts. It is never frantic, because the Brilliance Marketer knows his or her offer is sound and appealing and can afford to wait for customers to be ready to buy.

ABOUT CELIA ROCKS

Celia Rocks is president of Rocks-DeHart Public Relations , and author of Brilliance Marketing Management. Celia brings her own unique brand of resourcefulness and creativity to her public relations endeavors. Drawing on her 20 years of experience in the communications field, Celia's skill in marketing products, concepts, and ideas to worldwide audiences is enhanced by her bilingual (Spanish) ability and her multi-cultural orientation. Celia was an account supervisor and media specialist for Burson-Marsteller, the largest public relations firm in the world. Before joining Burson-Marsteller, Celia was also a producer for both Public Broadcasting and a CBS affiliate. You can reach her through www.brilliancemarketing.com.

CREATIVE PROSPECTING
CAN BE HALF THE FUN

CHAPTER IX.

Prospecting:
Catch & Release

There are huge fish in that pond.
Why accept minnows?

Kim DeMotte

> **"Prospecting. You don't have to like it,
> you just have to do it"**
> *Perry Tapp (My first corporate sales manager)*
>
> **"Real men prospect"**
> *Sign over Sales Manager's credenza*

John picked up the phone promptly at 9:00 Wednesday morning. In front of him was a list of several hundred prospective commercial service clients. He started to dial the phone, but found he needed to use the bathroom. By the time he had returned, having stopped by the coffee machine, it was already 9:19. He dialed the phone. Voice mail. He dialed again. Mr. Prospect was not in. He dialed a third time and talked with a receptionist, who told him his contact was in a meeting. Finally, at 9:32 he was talking to a real person. John asked if he could drive to the contact's place of business and help him with his telephone service. To his delight, the contact accepted and a date was set. John then filled in his report and refilled his coffee, and it was 9:52. By 10:00, John had dialed the phone six times and had one appointment. For his department, that's a pretty good average. This was John's report card from his boss. Dials to appointments; appointments to sales. It was John's job to do this every morning from 9:00 to 11:30. It was his PROSPECTING time.

PROSPECTING. The word strikes terror in the heart of almost every salesperson, be they virgin or veteran. Merriam-Webster's Collegiate® Thesaurus lists the following words as synonyms for the verb "prospect": explore, delve (into), dig (into), go (into), inquire (into), investigate, look (into), probe and sift. And here's the Merriam-Webster Collegiate® Dictionary definition of the verb "sell":

---

sell: to deliver or give up in violation of duty, trust, or loyalty : **BETRAY** – often used with *out*

a : to deliver into slavery for money **b :** to give into the power of another <*sold* his soul to the devil> **c :** to deliver the personal services of for money

: to dispose of or manage for profit instead of in accordance with conscience, justice, or duty <*sold* their votes>

: to impose on : **CHEAT**
a : to cause or promote the sale of <using television advertising to *sell* cereal> **b :** to make or attempt to make sales to **c :** to influence or induce to make a purchase

---

I find it interesting that this esteemed dictionary defines the verb "sell" with such negative terminology as "slavery," "betray" and "cheat" before it gets to the definition I choose to use. You thought you were in an admirable profession, didn't you?

The last definition of the verb "sell" – *a: to cause or promote the sale of <using television advertising to sell cereal> b: to make or attempt to make* *sales to c: to influence or induce to make a purchase* – is the one I will use in this discourse. In short, we perceive "prospecting" as probing and sifting, and "selling" as influencing or inducing to make a purchase. I want to make that distinction extremely clear. The two, although linked in the process of acquiring new business, are not the same thing. Prospecting is probing. Selling is influencing. Prospecting is sifting. Selling is inducing. They are very different skill sets. Not all salespeople are automatically endowed with both. (Some have neither!)

Most salespeople live for the day that they have a book of business that keeps them in their comfort zone 24/7. They have three to five (or 50 to 75, depending on the industry and market) clients they are responsible for, and the time consumed by "account maintenance" (schmoozing, customer relations, education, accounting, implementation meetings, route replenishment, etc.) leaves them with little or no time for acquiring new business. That's OK, because they're making their nut on the business they service. The individual salesperson may survive just fine in this mode. But can the company survive with all the sales staff coasting on existing business? I think not. Acquiring new customers is the life-sustaining duty of the sales force. New business is growth. New business is renewal. New business justifies budgets!

How can you make the Positive Power of NO work for this process? How can you use Limit Theory™ to improve prospecting? Remember, prospecting is sifting, it is the process of sorting out what is useful or valuable. It involves putting a set of things through a sieve to leave what is useful on one side and what is to be discarded on the other. If I want to collect rocks larger than one inch for my driveway, then I will put shovels full of rock-laden dirt in a sieve (such as a one-inch mesh screen) and shake it to let the unwanted sand and dirt drop away. What will be left are the rocks I need for my driveway, and the sand and dirt are easily disposed of. If I'm prospecting for gold, I put silty water from a creek bed into a pan and swish it around, allowing the heavier gold dust to fall to the bottom of the pan while the lighter silt particles float. The function of prospecting (sifting), is one of helping the worthless silt float away, letting the sand and dirt I *don't* need for my driveway accumulate to be easily hauled away.

How funny it is then, that we often hear the term "qualify" associated with the prospecting function. I submit that a person prospecting *cannot qualify anyone* or any company, any more than you can force useless silt to become gold dust, or sand to become one-inch rocks.

Sales managers do their sales process a gross injustice when they implore their charges to QUALIFY prospects. "Good morning, Mr. Silt. I think I'd like to qualify you as gold this morning. Whaddya say?" Prospects come to us with their own set of qualifications. In the case of gold prospecting, every speck in the pan is either useless silt or gold dust, period. No matter how much a salesperson considers himself or herself an alchemist, that useless silt cannot be changed into gold dust. The only *active* thing they can do (remember the words of Patrick Henry in chapter one, "The battle, sir, is not to the strong alone; it is to the vigilant, the *active*, the brave") is to quickly and decisively throw away the useless silt! The only way a gold prospector can improve the output of his process at any given location is to dip his pan into the water more frequently. If he can make $20 per hour dipping and sifting his pan 30 times each hour, then he can make $40 per hour dipping it 60 times. In order to dip more frequently, he must quickly dump the useless silt and dip again. If he wastes time looking at the silt, trying to decide if maybe one or two flecks of gold might not yet have found the bottom of his pan, he severely limits the number of times in an hour he can dip his pan. Consequently, he limits his income.

On my driveway project, I will find the correctly sized rocks I need more quickly by throwing shovelful of dirt after shovelful of dirt on the wire mesh, shaking it quickly and flipping the acceptable rocks over into the pile to be used.

What does sifting do? It quickly and efficiently eliminates anything that is not what we're looking for. In essence, our process is one of DIS-QUALIFICATION! Prospecting is all about DISQUALIFICATION!

What makes this function so efficient? In the above examples, we clearly know what we're looking for. We're looking for silt particles that are heavy enough to fall to the bottom of the pan, or rocks big enough to not fall through a one-inch mesh. And we're very clear about what we're NOT looking for. Our **Ideal Target** (Inside Front Cover) has reasonable, razor-sharp limits.

When we prospect for possible new business, are we that clear? Or do we prospect using an **Anything Goes Target** with a greatly enlarged bull's-eye? Maybe we purposefully enlarge the bull's-eye on the spot in order to accommodate our manager, who wants us to QUALIFY the prospect! I once asked a group of salespeople in a workshop if a particular business owner I had defined was a prospect for their company, and a voice from the back of the room asked, "Is he breathing?" Sometimes we want so much to QUALIFY a prospect that we too easily move our pre-determined limits so we can "get them in" the targeted subset we call "qualified." Sales management often exacerbates this situation by putting "Number of Qualified Prospects" or "Pipeline" into the formula by which a salesperson is paid!

What is the result of this flexibility? For one, the sales process is now burdened with prospects who are not gold, who will never be one-inch rocks, or who require a lot of expensive hand-holding while they possibly grow to be one-inch rocks. The sales force, in its zeal to QUALIFY prospects, may ask such questions as "Do you think you will ever, ever, ever need our widgets?" Then the prospect decides there is just no cost in saying maybe, or even yes. And the salesperson's heart grows lighter as he drives back to the office. "YES!" He tells himself. "I've got one!"

A publishing company I worked with had a direct mail database of about 14,000 organizations. They obtained these names over a 15-year period from various lists, association memberships, trade shows, etc. Every year, the company would send about $27 worth of direct mail to each of these names. People on the list would get brochures, invitations, newsletters and samples. Add that up. It's $378,000 in direct mail costs to "prospects." This list became the company's security blanket. As long as there were 14,000 names on that list, they had potential business out there! There were people the sales staff could talk to who were in the appropriate business and might need the company's services. Right?

In one 30-day telephone sampling of this database, the company discovered that 42% of these prospects either were out of business, had moved, no longer had a working phone number, or didn't have and never would have any use for my client's products or services. Some of the company's direct competitors were even on this list! Forty-two percent! They were spending $158,760 sending mail to people who weren't even there or would never need their product or service! (This was approximately a $6 million dollar company, so that represented more than 2.6% of gross sales). This was coming directly off the bottom line. Ouch!

So what does loosening the limits on prospect DISqualification cost? Could be $158,760 per year. In this case, the client was operating with an **Anything Goes Target**. Anyone who would fill out a bingo card at a trade show, belong to an association or was a charitable 501c(3) corporation was considered a prospect. To this company, the question "Is he a prospect?" was *always* answered by "Is he breathing?"

Overqualifying prospects has other, more subtle costs. They require more education. They need you to lower prices, arrange longer terms, build things that aren't stock items for you, and in general they eat up overhead.

In the "Good, Bad, and Ugly" chapter, you learned about deciding what to pursue and what not to pursue. You learned what products and services made sense, and what customers made sense. In this exercise, we will help you learn how to effectively filter the best prospects from your prospect lists so you make the best use of your time, money and other resources. Let's look at setting limits using some terms we've created. We'll use the LQ-EQ graph (Fig. 1) to determine what prospects FAIL TO DISQUALIFY themselves. We measure how LOGICALLY QUALIFIED a prospect is on the x-axis, and how EMOTIONALLY QUALIFIED a prospect is on the y-axis.

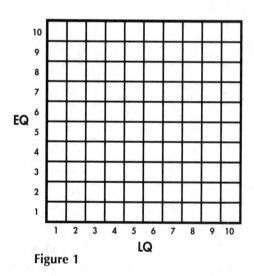

Figure 1

> **LOGICAL QUALIFICATION is a measurement of how much you (or your company) will have to bend (expand your bull's-eye) in order to do business with this prospect.**

Every prospect comes to us with an individual set of qualifications. Remember, this filtering process cannot QUALIFY a prospect. It can only DISQUALIFY a prospect based on where he falls on your target. He's either a bull's-eye or not a bull's-eye.

A Logically Qualified prospect is one who's still on your radar screen after you've mutually FAILED TO DISQUALIFY (the term we prefer to use as opposed to QUALIFY) each other. At Power of NO, we're not looking to QUALIFY prospects. We're looking for prospects that FAILED TO DISQUALIFY THEMSELVES. Logical Qualification asks the question "Where on my target does your arrow fall?" It doesn't ask "Where on my target might your arrow fall someday?" or "Where can I help you place your arrow?" or "Would you mind if I pulled out your arrow and placed it where I want it?"

There should be NO MANIPULATION in a question polling Logical Qualification. None. The prospect has a problem. Either you have the wherewithal to solve it, or you don't. In order for this prospect to FAIL TO DISQUALIFY himself, you will be totally capable of providing the resolution to his problem today. If you're not, then the prospect is DISQUALIFIED. It's because you don't want to bend (modify your business model, manufacturing process, financial requirements, etc.) to get the business. A clear limit exists between YES and NO. If that limit is not clear (and setting that limit and making it a sharp boundary is a management responsibility), you are operating with a **Big Fuzzy Target**, one with ill-defined boundaries, conditionally executed. And you probably are forced to work in arenas for which you are not best equipped. That can cause you problems with ramp-up time, your organization's learning curve, your supply chain, or worse.

the less "fit" you have, and the more you'll have to bend in order to get that business.

I'm totally aware that accommodating unique client needs is one way of diversifying and potentially growing your company. It's also the mantra of Customer Service. But I've seen these diversifications stretch engineering departments, purchasing agents, delivery managers and others to their wits' ends. If you're going to start making green widgets (and you don't make them now), then do so ON PURPOSE! Make it part of your plan. Assertively decide that getting into the Green Widget business is what you want to do and there are good valid reasons for doing so (besides accommodating a prospect in order to win this piece of business).

Please understand: The Positive Power of NO is not an enemy of change. It *IS* an enemy of change being directed at the whim of and held ransom by a piece of business or even an existing customer. Done on purpose and with adequate forethought, enlarging one's bull's-eye (but still keeping the limit between yellow and red very sharp) is perfectly valid, and even necessary. Being able to redesign your offer to solve 30 problems when it used to solve 20 is a good thing (if you can do so profitably). But this way, you get to pick which 10 solutions to add! Your prospect doesn't.

So we understand that there are prospects out there who are LOGICALLY QUALIFIED and others who aren't. How does the Catch & Release Prospecting Process filter those out? It asks the LOGICALLY DISQUALIFYING QUESTIONS first!

While it may seem like an obvious waste of time and effort, I have coached salespersons who would chase business before they even knew if the prospect *ever* bought what they sold! You've never done that, have you? Let's find that out first. "Do you ever buy widgets?" "Any plans to ever buy widgets?" Now, if the responses to these questions were NO, what would you do?

Some, because they've got a conversation going, would continue to tell their story, to build the value of widgets in the prospect's mind. And you know what? This approach will work once in a blue moon. That's a problem. It can grow to be a cancer on your sales process. It works just often enough that salespeople feel that they *should* spend time with UN-QUALIFIED PROSPECTS, CONVINCING them that their product or service has value for that prospect. But how much time, energy, effort, and money can be spent on CONVINCING unqualified prospects? More importantly, how many prospects have not been sorted and sifted in the meantime?

Remember, prospecting is sifting and sorting, not influencing and inducing! The object of sifting is to throw away the unproductive stuff. If there are un-interviewed prospects left in your database, you're statistically better off continuing the DISQUALIFICATION process on those than surgically attaching yourself to an UNQUALIFIED prospect who will listen. Out of your list of 1,000 prospects, 927 of them will never do business with you. When do you want to know which ones? RIGHT NOW! Ask them continuously. DISQUALIFY passionately. It's your job!

Traditional sales methodology would have us pontificate to the prospect. The hope is that we can raise the value in the prospect's mind to the point that it will be worth more to him than he has mentally budgeted. Frequently this has the salesperson continue to talk over the top of the prospect's demands to know "What does this cost?" If price is an object, why do you want to spend expensive selling time working with, educating and otherwise relating to a prospect who cannot or will not afford your product or service? Why not just ask, "How much have you budgeted for fixing this issue?" "What will you do if it comes out to cost more than that?" Your answer is most likely "Because he'll tell me he can't afford it and I'll lose him." FLASH! *YOU NEVER HAD HIM!*

If he can't afford to fix his problem with your solution, the only way you're going to get this piece of business is to lower your price (expand your bull's-eye) or begin the *I-CAN-CONVINCE-YOU* conversation. Is that what you want to do? I truly hope not. Someone out there needs your product or service and is willing to pay your price for it. Your job is to sift through the "NOes" until you find him.

EMOTIONAL QUALIFICATION is a measurement of how far your prospect has to bend (expand his bull's-eye) in order to do business with you.

We've successfully filtered out prospects that do not LOGICALLY qualify to do business with us. The rest are buyers, right? Not so fast. Just because they have FAILED TO DISQUALIFY themselves logically, doesn't mean they are ready to buy, or even ready to have you or a salesperson spend time, money and resources attempting to sell (induce, or influence) them anything.

For a myriad of reasons, a totally logically qualified prospect may not be EMOTIONALLY qualified. Perhaps he's totally satisfied with his current source. Perhaps he buys from his brother-in-law. Perhaps his current supplier offers services (such as inventory management, on-time delivery, local warehousing, extended credit terms or engineering consulting) that you do not offer. Perhaps your relationship-building skills have failed and he just doesn't like you (that's an emotional reason!). Or he just really likes the other guy.

Just as on the LOGICAL QUALIFICATION scale, on the scale of EMOTIONAL QUALIFICATION from 1 to 10, you want to spend your time, money and other resources on prospects that exist at the higher end.

This is where my treatise on relationship building comes in. We hear so much today in the Sales Training arena about building relationships with our customers and prospects. I couldn't agree more.

I will suggest, however, that investing the social, emotional, or financial capital in building relationships with Low LQ prospects is a waste of time. But what about low EQ prospects? It depends on the available resources and the prospect pool you are working with. Let's look at Figure 3.

Prospects who buy what you sell in large enough quantities (have LOGICALLY FAILED TO DISQUALIFY THEMSELVES), may have many reasons to buy or not to buy from you. Their EMOTIONAL QUALIFICATION is usually in flux. On Monday, they are totally pleased with their current supplier. EQ = 1. On Tuesday, that incredibly competent supplier delivers the

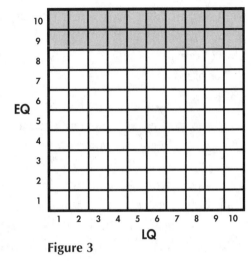

Figure 3

wrong order to his door, and demands COD because his accounting department has screwed up. Is his EQ still 1? I doubt it. It could be more like a 5 or 6. But what makes a prospect a 9 or 10? How important is this issue? Is it life threatening? EQ = 10. Can he buy this stuff anywhere? EQ = 1.

While the LQ scale is concrete and quantifiable, the EQ scale is subjective. It's the part of the relationship that asks, "How does the prospect feel about doing business with you, and does he or she have any compelling reasons to buy from you or not to buy from you?" Prospects usually cannot (or will not) share with you enough information to assess their EQ accurately. At the highest levels, (bleeding on the sidewalk and gasping for breath) they may let their guard down and share with you details about the miserable behavior of their existing supplier. You can interpret that as EQ = 9+. But for the most part, in the prospecting phase of the selling process we can only ask how important changing vendors, or fixing this problem, really is. We could get answers ranging from "not very important" to "mission critical."

After hearing your offer, and after failing to disqualify himself logically, if a prospect's EQ response is in the range of "not very important," his EQ is probably not very high. If he was desperate to solve a problem, don't you think he'd share that with you? If he wouldn't, then he's playing some sort of game with you or asking to be convinced. You (with your newfound ability pick the type of business you want to do) can see that kind of prospect in the red ring of your bull's-eye and execute the Positive Power of NO.

Are some prospects perfect fits? Their needs are tailor-made to your offer, and they have a desperate need for your services now? You bet. And you **_do_** bet. Every day you're in business. If you don't believe that prospects with LQ = 10 **_and_** EQ = 10 are out there in your prospect world somewhere, I suggest you alter your business until your offer identifies High LQ prospects. This is a problem that needs to be addressed in Strategic Planning. What business should we NOT be in? One that has no (or too few) LOGICALLY QUALIFIED PROSPECTS? One with whom no one wants or needs to do business?

The world is full of companies who keep inventing what they believe to be better mousetraps even though there is a plethora of perfectly good traps on the market. Your market area may or may not have enough mice to support a population of LOGICALLY QUALIFIED prospects. It also may or may not have too many vendors and solution sources to negatively affect your prospect's ability to be EMOTIONALLY QUALIFIED.

When prospects hit our radar screen, they arrive with their own Logical and Emotional Qualification numbers. You have to bend more or less to get the business and they have to bend more or less to do business with you.

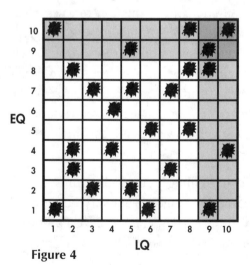

Figure 4

In the example in Figure 4, 24 prospects have passed through our DISQUALIFICATION process. Five of them had LQ's of 9 or 10. Of those five, one had an EQ of 1. Perhaps his warehouse was full of product and he bought it all from his brother-in-law and executed a standing contract good for the next 10 years. He's LOGICALLY QUALIFIED and EMOTIONALLY DISQUALIFIED. Another of those five had an EQ of 4. Perhaps he has a supplier, not a relative, who takes good care of him MOST of the time and whose prices are USUALLY OK. He's indicated that he wants you to send him a catalog. Do you spend time money and effort building a close relationship with this prospect? Probably not. But there's enough potential that you probably should send the catalog and continue the process of DISQUALIFYING. Is this one you pass on to your sales staff? Probably not. A third one of these has an EQ of 8. Hmmmmm. This is a tough one. It's not a 9. But it's sooooooo close! Couldn't we just pass this one over to the sales staff and hope they can do something with him? Maybe they can hang on until he becomes a 9. If your cutoff is 9 or above, then 8 must be a "NO." If you as a company want to include 8's, then drop the limit to 8. But do it ON PURPOSE! Don't let your sales staff (or your hunger for a deal, any deal) make that decision for you. As long as the limit is set at 9 or above, then the 8 is a "NO." More about this later....

How about those that are EMOTIONALLY QUALIFIED at 9 or above? Likewise, we have five of them. Of those, three are "ready and willing to buy" but are not a true "fit" for your offer. Their LQ's fall below your predetermined threshold. In order to do business with them, you or your company will have to bend and alter your product or service. A good example of this is a current "Raving Fan" client who, because of your excellent relationship, wants you to build, engineer or acquire something you do not already do and for which you have no plans. If you're not ready for that, there is only one response. I'd suggest helping him find a reliable source rather than altering your whole business to accommodate this request. If you are, I hope you at least make that decision (again) ON PURPOSE.

Then there are the two who FAIL TO DISQUALIFY themselves on both scales. VOILA! These are the ones you've been looking for! Their LQ is 9 or 10, so you will not have to alter your offering to solve their issues or accommodate their needs. Their EQ is 9 or 10, so they are ready, willing and able to resolve these issues quickly – without having to "bend" to do business with you.

Do you have to be so selective? No. It depends on the limits you set. Remember, you set these limits in defense of your strategic directives. If you have the resources to develop relationships with prospects who don't yet buy what you sell, and it's OK, then go ahead. If you have the sales staff skilled enough to help a prospect understand that his EQ is not a 6, but actually a 7 (see the following chapter on the Positive Power of NO and selling), then, by all means, set the EQ limits lower. If you set both your LQ and EQ limits at 5, for example, and only spent your sales system resources on prospects who arrived in the upper right 25% of the LQ-EQ graph, what would that mean to your sales? (Figure 5). And if you did nothing more than NEVER spend system resources on the lower left 25%, would that improve the effectiveness of your sales process?

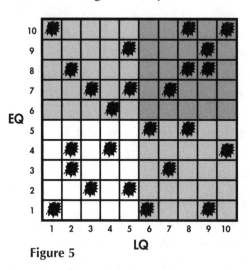

Figure 5

When should you consider moving the limits? Moving the LQ limits is most often a function of return on investment (ROI) of resources invested in the sales process. Moving the LQ limit, say from 9 down to 6, means that more prospects will FAIL TO DISQUALIFY themselves, and they will represent a family of prospects that are not as potentially 'productive' (profitable) as those with LQs of 9 and up. Why would I want to do this? You might want to do this because your prospecting system is not finding enough LQ's = 9 or above to keep producing (or servicing) at capacity. If you lower your LQ limit, and begin to sell to lower LQ clients, you'll have to decide whether or not you can make an adequate living supplying these prospect's needs. Or you may have to modify your delivery (manufacturing, service offer, etc.) to maintain profitability. You may want to consider reducing your sales force as an alternative if the LQ = 9+'s are producing good enough results.

But let's say we're getting a lot of requests for bids on green widgets. So far, we have allowed green widget buyers to DISQUALIFY themselves because we don't make green widgets. We can make the decision to go into the green widget business, but again, we should do it *on purpose*. If we relax the limits, it should not be for one or two prospects, but because we think there's an untapped niche and we can budget for a green paint line and make it work from a strategic point of view. Likewise, we may find that a limit of annual business of $50,000 is so tight that we only find one every two years. So we might decide to lower that limit and design methods to handle $30,000 customers more profitably – ON PURPOSE! Moving the LQ limits, then, is purely a function of a strategic decision to bend our offer to meet a family of prospects' needs ON PURPOSE!

When should we move the EQ limit? Where to set the EQ limit is a function of the skill set of your sales force. How are they at getting a prospect to understand the level of his need? Depending on the skills of the sales person, an EQ of 9 for some might be an EQ of 6 for others. It's a degree of perceived readiness. And some sales people are better at helping the prospect see his readiness than others. Working with prospects on getting them to understand their level of need is where inducing and influencing begin. It's where the DISQUALIFICATION ends and the SELLING begins.

OTHER RESOURCES

David H. Sandler: You Can't Teach a Kid to Ride a Bike at a Seminar; Bay Head Publishing, Stevenson Maryland, 1999.

Jacques Werth and Nicholas E. Ruben: High Probability Selling Reinvents the Selling Process[SM]; ABBA Publishing Company, Dresher, Pennsylvania, 1999.

*   *   *   *   *   *   *

i   Blanchard, Kenneth. *Raving Fans: A Revolutionary Approach to Customer Service.* (William Morrow & Co: New York).

179

ABOUT KIM DeMOTTE

Kim DeMotte is the founder and managing partner of Power of NO, LLC, a consulting consortium specializing in improving management effectiveness. For the past seven years, he has worked with companies and their leadership teaching them why, when, where and how to say "NO" to keep their strategic plans on track. His clients range from Fortune 100 AT&T to sole proprietorships.

Having started his adult life aiming to be an engineer like his father, Kim soon gravitated toward human sciences and completed his bachelor's and master's degrees in psychology.

He has been selling something or managing the selling of something for more than thirty-five years. He's sold intangibles, metal products, musical instruments, computer hardware, software and consulting services. He's owned a manufacturing company, a distributorship, two service companies, a software company, and now a consultancy. He's managed sales organizations for manufacturers, publishers, and service organizations. He's done it all....WRONG! But he's educable!

He resides in Webster Groves, Missouri, a bustling, turn-of-the-last-century suburb of St. Louis.

DON'T WORRY HAROLD,
WE'RE BOTH MASTERS
AT TRADIN' AND MAKIN' DEALS.

CHAPTER X.

Power of NO Selling: Tradin' and Makin' Deals

David Allen

TRADIN' AND MAKIN' DEALS

Grandpa went to the small town of Keota, Iowa, every Saturday morning to "do some tradin' and makin' deals." Grandpa was both buying and selling; he was tradin'. At the Keota Produce he traded eggs for chicken feed. At the market he traded fresh vegetables for flour and sugar. On the way home he stopped at a neighboring farm to make a deal with Elmer Waller. Grandpa wanted more piglets to fatten and take to market. Elmer needed a male hog with "good blood" to father good quality piglets. Grandpa traded the use of his prize-winning male hog for the biggest litter of the resulting baby pigs from all of Elmer's sows. It was a good deal for both of them.

Grandpa and Elmer were masters at tradin' and makin' deals. They grew up together. They treated each other with integrity. They knew they would be fair with each other as they had been in the many deals they'd made over the years. They made the deal in a very honest and direct way. They were concerned for each other's freedom to decide or make a choice about making the deal; they didn't push each other. They knew they could and would say NO to each other if the deal did not fit. They understood each other's issues and emotions. They knew each other's readiness to make a deal. Elmer and Grandpa did not talk each other into "buying" anything. They would not make a deal unless it completely satisfied the logical and emotional issues for both of them. This was a good trade.

Grandpa and Elmer understood the importance of making decisions and moving on, even if it meant not making the deal. They both needed to find out whether the deal was going to work sooner rather than later. They didn't have time to waste waiting for each other. If the deal wasn't right for either of them, they wanted to move to the next possibility.

Tradin' and makin' deals is a good model for 21st century selling. Tradin' and makin' deals doesn't have the same negative baggage associated with the word "selling." Modern selling is not one-sided. Modern selling is a mutual process of discovery. When tradin' and makin' deals, NO deal is the best choice if the parties don't find a fit.

Buying/selling is the art of mutual agreement and commitment. It's an organized, mutually agreed upon process between buyers and sellers that achieves a mutually agreed upon trade. Selling is the process of discovering the emotional and logical reasons to decide whether or not to make a deal.

There was buying and selling going on Saturday morning. Grandpa was engaged in the process of facilitating decisions to make mutually beneficial exchanges of goods, services and ideas. He was an expert at developing and discovering mutual Logical and Emotional Qualifications (LQ and EQ) with a trading partner.

Grandpa was a prospector, too. He sifted through the whole neighborhood looking for someone logically and emotionally qualified to use his male hog in trade for some pigs. He certainly did not have an **Anything Goes Target** (see inside front cover) when it came to his prize hog. Some neighbors were not logically qualified because they did not have any sows. Others had sows but didn't understand that good genetics make better pigs. Some who were logically qualified were not emotionally qualified because they did not have enough mutual trust or they did not like the color of Grandpa's male hog.

After Elmer had failed to disqualify himself, the prospecting ended and the selling began. What were the emotional factors that determined whether they would trade? What were the logical factors? Elmer and Grandpa had to work through the discovery process to make the deal.

Grandpa had a problem. He wanted more piglets to fatten. Elmer had a problem. He needed a male hog to breed his sows. They had each other's solutions – the perfect deal.

Both Are Seller and Both Are Buyer

When "tradin' and makin' deals," the roles of the buyer and the seller become the same. The deal or trade is clearly mutual, it's fair and it's win-win. The **Ideal Targets** of both parties overlap or they simply would not do the deal.

The buyer and seller together must discover the match of their **Ideal Targets**. Selling and buying is the same process. It's a matter of mutual communication. It's a matter of turning over every rock, looking for reasons and emotions to disqualify each other. If the **Ideal Targets** are not a match, the sooner we know that, the better. It's a matter of making a choice, a decision. It's a matter of taking action. Both are the role of the seller and both are the role of the buyer. We sell the way we buy and we buy the way we sell.

Some deals and trades are simple and straightforward, like the one between Grandpa and Elmer. Most are not. Buying/selling is generally a complex interaction because sellers cannot clearly identify their **Ideal Targets** and because the buyer's bull's-eye does not always fit the seller's bull's-eye. Sellers and buyers are suggesting to each other that they change their targets. That's negotiation.

Sellers are making business decisions to change and refine their bull's-eyes as the process moves along. Changing the bull's-eye is a serious business decision. Such changes must be made within the guidelines established by the corporate business strategy. Sales people have rules to follow and formal processes to use in order to revise the offerings. When new situations come up, new strategic solutions are needed. These situations require decisions by people empowered to make strategic changes. The process is dynamic.

If the buyer's bulls-eye does not seem to fit the seller's bull's-eye, the seller's role is to help the buyer discover changes that can be made so that the fit improves. The major role of the seller is to help the buyer discover his or her Emotional Qualification. This is fundamentally a communications process, similar to the way a personal counselor might help someone discover and express his or her emotions. The more the buyers realize that their emotions are higher than they originally thought, the higher the EQ. In order to discover EQ effectively, product knowledge, communication skills, counseling skills and a general understanding of human psychology and human nature come into play. Power of NO selling is counSELLing.

There are two ways a seller and a buyer can make a deal when their bull's-eyes do not overlap or match. One way is for the seller to enlarge his bull's-eye to encompass the buyer's. Typically this is the seller "bending" his offer to accommodate the low LQ of the buyer (recall the definition of Logical Qualification). Could be pricing. Could be delivery terms. Could be product or service offered. The other way is for the buyer to recognize that his EQ is higher than he originally perceived when he established his bull's-eye. For example, the buyer may not have realized what impact his current solution has on his profitability, HR issues or re-work when he established his bull's-eye. Sellers should not change their offers easily (expand that bull's-eye) to accommodate the LQ of the buyer. Sellers must master the communication strategies and techniques that help the buyer understand the true level of his EQ, so that the buyer is open to change.

Some sellers fear that that discovery of the buyer's emotions will lead to disqualification. Indeed, this is possible. The emotional aspects of the process can be taken too far. Some buyers resent sharing their emotions while others are embarrassed by the emotions they express, thus lowering their EQ's due to trust and comfort issues. Sellers must be skilled at knowing when the EQ is at its optimum to make the deal.

There is a third choice when either the seller or the buyer discovers the offer is not a fit; disqualification or NO deal. While you might think disqualification or NO deal is a poor option, a changed seller's offer without adequate strategic forethought can be disastrous, and a buyer with an artificially high EQ can eventually regret the purchase.

Sellers must always look for ways to adapt their products, services or ideas to the marketplace. But changes to the offering should be made only after careful thought in accordance with strategic management and corporate guidelines. Sales people alone should not make strategic changes in the company's offering. For example, a seller promises two-day delivery when the company policy and practice is three days. This business promise may have far-reaching ramifications for the company. There often are "unique opportunities" or "good reasons" but the seller alone should not make a decision to change the **Ideal Target**.

The higher a buyer's Emotional Qualification, the more flexibility that buyer has when considering solutions that fit his or her Logical Qualification requirements. EQ is the degree of flexibility in the buyer. For example, trust is usually an important EQ factor. The greater the trust (EQ factor), the more likely the buyer is to change specifications to meet the seller's offerings. Elmer trusted (EQ) Grandpa when Grandpa told him that his red boar would be better than the black and white one that Elmer had in mind as his bull's-eye. Elmer changed his mind because he trusted (EQ) Grandpa's expertise and advice. The degree to which Elmer was willing to change was a measure of his EQ.

Logical Qualification and Emotional Qualification are tools for tradin' and makin' deals. Neither party has an advantage over the other. Furthermore, if one party doesn't understand the other's LQ and EQ, communication becomes more difficult. Superior understanding does not give either side an advantage over the other. LQ and EQ cannot be used against you. Tradin' and makin' deals with all parties understanding one another is simply more honest and efficient.

Power-of-NO Selling is very efficient and effective for everyone involved. How can you use it in today's sophisticated business transactions? Achieving Power-of-NO Selling requires a non-traditional point of view, a non-traditional communication strategy and non-traditional tactics.

TRADITIONAL SELLER VS. BUYER

Six-year-old Steven came to the door fund-raising for the school library, selling an entertainment coupon book. He had his bike helmet on and a little wet spot on his shirt under his chin. See, it's hard to talk without slobbering when you're that age and your front teeth are missing. He was a traditionally trained sales person. He launched right into one of the nicest little presentations that you could imagine. He was positive and enthusiastic. He had the I-can–convince-you attitude. He knew a benefit and feature of the coupon book: "It's for the school library" and "You get free stuff." I was impressed. It was all seller-centered, as you would expect of a six-year-old. I was not a participant in the process. This was not a mutual selling process. Steven was the seller and I was the buyer. He was influencing and inducing. Seller vs. buyer. This is traditional selling. It resulted in a sale for Steven this time.

I bought! Why? Because I had an **Anything Goes Target** with no clear boundaries or rules. I don't use coupon books. My LQ was low. On the other hand, I was emotionally qualified, a "10." His helmet, wet shirt, presentation and the library struck an emotional chord in me. I failed to disqualify myself because my high EQ allowed me to modify my LQ (which modified my bull's-eye). But as a buyer, I soon tire of this kind of transaction. It was a win/lose deal. The next time I won't buy unless, of course, the emotion thing happens again and my target again reverts to **Anything Goes**. This was not Power-of-NO Selling.

Traditional selling encourages sellers to ignore the balance between Emotional Qualification and Logical Qualification. This is what Steven did with me. He was unaware and didn't care that I was not Logically Qualified. However, my low Logical Qualification will make me a one-time buyer. I still don't use coupon books! One-time buyers who are not Logically Qualified are not what most sellers are looking for.

The roles of buyer and seller are not the same in traditional selling. Traditionally the seller is the aggressor and the buyer is the defender. The seller tells and the buyer defends with objections. The seller is doing the act of selling to the buyer. The seller is pushing, presenting solutions, influencing and inducing. The buyer is naturally resisting the transaction because of the emotional disconnect. The buyer and seller are not equal partners in communication.

Traditional selling exaggerates the positive. Buyers generally choose a negative position for self protection. They suspect that the sellers are being overly positive to cover up the negatives of their offerings.

The traditional sales manager's mantra of "be positive, be enthusiastic" is intended to stampede the buyer to high Emotional Qualification. Buyers resist because they don't want to be emotionally manipulated into making decisions without a rational or logical component.

Be careful! Being "positive" and "enthusiastic" frequently causes sellers to get caught up in their own positive emotions. Then they can surrender to the temptation of a Steven-like "I-can-convince-you" conversation. These things look artificial and insincere, which lowers the buyer's EQ. Power-of-NO Selling is not aggressive, pushy, overly positive or overly enthusiastic. It is mutual, rational, logical, non-emotional, open and fair.

Traditional selling philosophy, strategies and techniques have created an adversarial relationship between buyers and sellers. Traditional buying/selling subverts good communication. It offers solutions without problems, it offers misleading information to gain advantage and it manipulates the emotions. One party is assuming qualification while the other is assuming disqualification. It is not a mutual communication process; it's a struggle for advantage and control. It's who has the cleverest comeback. It's a contest of who can tweak whom first.

Both parties have developed defense mechanisms to protect themselves. Each party tends to withhold important information and even lie a little sometimes. Traditionally the buyer's agenda is to gather information about the seller and the seller's offering while skipping or avoiding talk about disqualification. The buyer tempts the seller into providing information and solutions, even consulting services, before the completion of the disqualification process. Traditional sellers are eager to participate. They are eager to provide "bids" and "proposals" based on incomplete LQ and EQ information. "Requests for proposal" do not provide any EQ information and they frequently give incomplete, inaccurate or uninformed LQ information. Dumping information and solutions prior to an EQ disqualification process is not relevant and usually only partially valuable to the buyer. It's a waste of time and it causes poor business decisions. Traditional selling can be a dysfunctional system.

Many books have been written on getting to YES. Traditional sellers push for YES answers. They ask loaded questions, such as, "Would you like to save some money?" Or, "If I could show you a way to earn more money or increase profits would you give me 30 minutes?" Buyers resist because they feel pressure to give up their uniquely human choice of NO. They are put off by the lack of integrity. They are afraid of losing control.

Power-of-NO Selling cuts through the traps of traditional selling because NO is OK. NO is a good choice. NO is a good decision. Disqualification is good. Power-of-NO Selling focuses on the NO choices, not on "getting to yes."

Power-of-NO Selling is not only buyer-centered. Nor is the burden of the buying/selling process all on the seller's shoulders. The burden is shared. If a buyer does not want to share in the process, he can disqualify himself. It's not about buyer first or seller first. Both sellers and buyers recognize that they can end the process at any time. Of course, the seller is interested in the problems, needs and concerns of the buyer. The buyer must be willing to participate equally. Power-of-NO Selling is mutually centered selling.

THE POWER-OF-NO SELLING ATTITUDE

Power-of-NO Selling takes courage and integrity. The communication techniques and skills are not standard, traditional selling techniques. They are counter intuitive to many people. The techniques sound like the seller is helping the buyer say NO. Indeed, Power-of-NO Sellers are looking for reasons not to make the deal. It exposes the pitfalls and the obstacles very openly. It encourages buyers to disqualify themselves. It gets quickly to the EQ issues.

The Power-of-No Seller must have the courage to share control of the communication process with the buyer, while being very careful not to give away control. The seller must be careful to lead the process, but not dictate the process. The seller must not tell the buyer the rules and agenda of the process but rather mutually agree on the rules and agenda. However, the buyer must agree to some of the Power-of-NO Seller's rules and agenda for the buyer to be Logically Qualified. The buyer and the seller must move along together. Both must understand a time reference, a budget or financial reference, and a decision process or criteria reference. It's a matter of mutuality. It's a matter of integrity, choice and courage.

Power-of-NO Selling focuses on raising the buyer's perceived Emotional Qualification. It's all about the buyer's emotions. The Power-of-NO Seller is looking for negative emotions such as fear, anger, embarrassment, loss of self-esteem and loss of "face," and for positive emotions including joy, caring for others, pleasure, self-esteem and power. When using Power-of-NO Selling the seller openly encourages discussion of emotions both positive and negative. The seller has no fear of exposing the buyer's emotions because she understands the power of a high EQ.

The buyer comes to the process with a natural tendency to avoid EQ. People are afraid of exposing personal emotions to others. It's human nature. The greater the trust between buyer and seller, the more likely the buyer is to disclose his EQ accurately. Building trust and asking the EQ questions is the expertise of the Power-of-NO Seller.

A Power-of-NO Seller is not emotionally involved with the buyer. NO Sellers must have very firm control over their own emotions, even as the buyers become emotional. During the Emotional Qualification raising process, the seller must have the self-control to not avoid the negative emotions of the buyer. When the buyer becomes excited and enthusiastic, the seller must have the self-control to avoid becoming emotionally excited. When sellers become emotionally involved in the buy/sell process, they tend to lose control and retreat to the traditional I-can-convince-you process.

NO is choice. There is a strong attitude that arises out of free will. Buyers are afraid of losing the NO option. Power-of-NO Sellers help buyers keep NO as a viable alternative through the entire buying/selling process. By doing this, the seller removes the buying pressure and maintains leadership of a balanced communication process.

Many bad experiences have happened when a buyer or seller should have said NO but didn't. These occasional bad buy/sell experiences are very powerful. Buyers have been psychologically conditioned from the bad experiences when the sellers take advantage of buyers. A few bad sellers have been there before you. The buyer is conditioned to worry about being "pushed" to yes. This conditioning results in the buyer protecting her choice to say NO. Buyers and sellers feel guilty because they didn't say NO when they should have. I should have said NO to Steven. Furthermore, we are often embarrassed by the results of the buying/selling process. We paid more than someone else or we bought something that we didn't need.

The word NO traditionally disappoints people. NO hurts people's feelings, makes them mad and causes conflict. Sellers must have the self-confidence and self-control to deal with the emotions of the word NO. In order to be effective, the seller must maintain an emotional separation or distance, much like that of a psychologist or therapist. The buy/sell process flies out of control when the seller loses control emotionally. Sellers tend to avoid NO because of the associated emotional disappointment. Rising above this is perhaps the most difficult test of the seller's self-control.

The EQ is the hard part of the buy/sell communication. People have a hard time sorting out facts from emotion. Logical Qualification is a factual process. Logical Qualification is discovering facts and limits. It is or it isn't. It is a mutual exchange. It should be easy, but it isn't. Selling from NO sounds different to the buyer. The seller phrases questions differently and responds to questions differently.

It's paradoxical. NO and YES both have bad reputations. A person who agrees quickly is called a "yes man" and is disrespected because his need for approval from others may be bigger than his personal integrity. He has an **Anything Goes Target**. On the other hand, naysayers (who have **Anal Targets**) say NO to almost everything and are disrespected because they are inflexible, rebellious or pessimistic. A seller using negative words recklessly risks being seen as an unprofessional naysayer. The traditional seller who refuses to take NO for an answer or pushes toward YES becomes a "pushy salesperson" who is disrespected and not trusted by buyers.

Every seller has a unique communication style. One person's words, tone and body language will send a completely different message when mimicked. The dialogues that follow are not to be used as scripts, nor are they to be mimicked. These exact words may work only for this author. Take these words as examples. Become aware of the rules. Create language that fits for you. The concept is to help the buyer understand that his EQ might be higher than he first thought.

> **EMOTIONAL QUALIFICATION is a measurement of how far your prospect has to bend (extend his bull's-eye) in order to do business with you.**

In this exercise, the seller is helping the buyer reduce the amount he/she might need to bend in order to do business with you.

Power-of-NO Selling is different, so don't predict responses and results from the buyer. Be very careful. First attempts at NO Selling are uncomfortable.

The Power-of-NO Seller has made an appointment with a prospect who failed to disqualify herself over the phone. After polite greetings, here's the conversation.

Seller: Before we get started, I need your help. We don't know whether or not there are mutually acceptable reasons for us to do business. So let's do this, if it's OK with you. Let's look for reasons why we might not be able to do business. When either of us discovers a compelling reason why we should not continue, let's tell each other right away and end the conversation. Is that fair or not?

Buyer: What do you mean?

Seller: Well, we can both think of a number of reasons why we don't have a match, so let's ask each other some questions, and stop when either of us sees there isn't a match. Is that fair?

Buyer: OK, so what do you do again?

Seller: That's a good place to start. And after that, we'll talk about your situation, your issues and goals. Then let's cover the time, money and other commitments we can make. Next, we need to understand and agree with each other's decision process to take action. If we're still tracking, we'll talk about solutions. Is that fair or not?

Buyer: Sounds good. So what do you do?

Seller: We sell printing and printing services that add efficiencies and profits to organizations that are not totally satisfied with their current vendor's quality or delivery options. I don't know if any of this applies to your situation or not. Can I ask you, what is your present situation with printing and printing services?

Does this sound like the beginning of a traditional buy/sell conversation, or is it different? Are sellers comfortable or uncomfortable with it? Is it courageous, honest and open? Is it a little cheeky? Is it fair and professional or pushy? Is it emotional or rational? Is there an agenda that's hidden from the buyer or not? Is the seller digging a hole to fall in later, or is the seller on solid ground? Does the buyer "get it"? Is a process starting or not? Is there a strategy in the open or is it hidden? Are they gaining or losing mutual trust? Are they going to waste time? Is the seller's message consistent or inconsistent? Is the seller behaving ethically or is there doubt about that?

For many people this conversation is counterintuitive, upside-down and backward. That's the way of Power-of-NO Selling.

Rule: Be gentle and direct.

Power-of-NO Selling is direct and gentle. It's direct because sellers help buyers disqualify themselves quickly and efficiently. It's gentle to keep the buyer from being afraid of direct, NO-oriented communication. The seller must "listen" to the buyer's body language, tone of voice and words to "hear" discomfort or aggravation with the communication. Any discomfort must be addressed immediately, gently and directly.

Seller: Before we get started, I need your help. (The tone is soft and the pace is slow; the whole approach is gentle so the seller doesn't come off as a naysayer.) We don't know whether or not there are mutually acceptable reasons for us to do business (direct). … So let's do this if it's OK with you (gentle). Let's look for reasons why we might not be able to do business (direct). When either one of us discovers a compelling reason why we should not continue, let's tell each other right away and end the conversation (sharp-edged, direct). Is that fair or not? (gentle).

Buyer: OK, so what do you do again?

Seller: That's a good place to start. And after that, (use a calm tone, not overly confident … even a little hesitant, gentle) we'll talk about your situation, your issues and goals.

Rule: Deal with the emotion first.

Selling/buying is a non-emotional process for the seller and an emotional process for the buyer. The seller struggles to be non-emotional in an emotion-laden process. Selling from NO gives the seller a completely rational position. Once committed to the NO Selling process, the difficulty is mastering the technique of dealing with emotion without becoming emotionally involved.

The purpose is to get the emotions out in the open. This process leads to the discovery of Emotional Qualifications. Any avoidance of emotions leads the buyer to hide his emotions, making the discovery of EQ more difficult.

Buyer: I'm really piled up. Our systems went down this morning.

Seller: Looks like you're upset (very gentle). Maybe I should come back another time.

Buyer: Well ... let's go ahead, you're here.

Seller: You still seem preoccupied with it. We can reschedule if that would help (this gives the other person time to settle down and get prepared emotionally).

Buyer: No. I'm OK now. What was it we were going to talk about?

Rule: No Need for Approval.

Sellers must overcome their need for approval. NO does not satisfy our need for approval and our avoidance of rejection. NO Selling is not the traditional way of selling nor is it generally expected by buyers. NO Selling seems to be inviting rejection, when in fact it is defending the free will of the buyer.

Buyer: I'm really piled up. Our systems went down this morning.

Seller: Looks like you're upset (very gentle). Maybe I should come back another time (invite NO).

Buyer: Well ... let's go ahead, you're here.

Seller: You still seem preoccupied with it. We can reschedule if that would help (invite NO again to give them time to settle down)?

Buyer: No. I'm OK now. What was it we were going to talk about?

Rule: When asked the right "NO Selling" question, the buyer does not end the process when given the choice to do so.

"NO Selling" is a counterintuitive technique of communication. The Seller intentionally presents the communication from the NO point of view. This is the opposite of traditional selling behavior. The buyer is intentionally presented with the NO option. The buyer feels no pressure and has no reason to be defensive. The buyer does not respond by saying NO automatically in order to protect himself from an aggressive, pushy, traditional seller.

Buyers tend to respond to sellers' offer of the NO choice with openness. Buyers respond to the seller's integrity with integrity and to the seller's courage with courage. The buyer and the seller both have the integrity and courage to communicate accurately.

Two things happen in "NO Selling." First, the seller offers to logically or emotionally disqualify the buyer by offering the NO option. The buyer either agrees to the disqualification or declines to be disqualified. It's direct and efficient.

Secondly, the seller is giving the buyer permission and even encouraging a NO response. NO selling is very gentle and reassuring for the buyer. The buyer usually declines the opportunity to say NO because he feels safe. The communication continues.

> Seller: We sell printing and printing services that add efficiencies and profits to organizations that are not totally satisfied with their current vendor's quality or delivery options. I don't know if any of this applies to your situation ("NO Selling"). Can I ask you, (gentle) what is your present situation with printing and printing services? (Direct) I would guess you are perfectly satisfied ("NO Selling")?
>
> Buyer: Right now we have a provider that we like. We don't need your services.

Seller: Oh, OK, I understand (gentle). There are a number of good providers in the market. Before we end this, ("NO Selling") can I ask (gentle), What do you really like about your present provider ("NO Selling")?

Buyer: Sure, they…. (and the interview continues).

Rule: Never be defensive.

Buyers and traditional sellers are defensive. The amateur sales people before us have trained buyers to protect themselves from sellers. Many buyers lack the courage to say NO, so they avoid clear answers. As a defense mechanism, they abandon their integrity to get rid of sales people with false NO's, or they use a false yes to take advantage of the seller's expertise by getting free advice in bids and proposals. Some form of "maybe" is an indicator of a defensive buyer. Sellers become defensive by talking too much and reverting to the I-can-convince-you mode. They tend to defend their offer in seller-based terms.

Seller: We sell printing and printing services that add efficiencies and profits to organizations that are not totally satisfied with their current vendor's quality or delivery options. I don't know if any of this applies to your situation. Can I ask you, what is your present situation with printing and printing services?

Buyer: Well (huffy tone), we're happy, if you don't have anything better for me let's not waste time.

Seller: I can see I've upset you (deal with emotion). I apologize (not defensive). Would it be OK if I tried to rephrase that (gentle)? I don't want to assume that we have products and services that fit your situation, without a better understanding (direct). Does that make better sense (gentle)?

Rule: Mutual agreement.

Buyers and sellers agree on the next steps in the process as they go. They move along together. The consistent option of NO has created the trust that gives the buyer and the seller confidence to proceed to the discovery of EQ.

> Seller: I suspect we can both think of a number of reasons why we don't have a fit ("NO Selling"), so let's ask each other some questions (mutual agreement) and stop when either of sees there isn't a match. Is that fair (mutual agreement)?
>
> Buyer: I was hoping you would give me a proposal.
>
> Seller: Help me a minute (gentle). We need to talk about that (not defensive). Is that fair (mutual)? I don't know if this will work for you (NO Selling). Before my company agrees to prepare a proposal or a bid we need to have clear and mutual understanding that we can do business together in principle (direct). Can we talk about your issues, goals, problems and concerns to see if we really qualified for each other (mutual)? If we can agree in principle, what's next?

Rule: Ask questions to find the EQ.

The goal of EQ questions is to help the buyer become aware of the emotions behind the problems, issues, concerns and goals. Buyers generally do not share emotions quickly. A series of questions is generally required. The seller asks for facts to gain an understanding before asking about the buyer's emotions. Typical questions are about details, frequency, examples and attempted solutions.

As the buyer reviews his issues with the seller, the seller skillfully keeps the buyer on target, constantly giving him permission to say NO. The buyer feels no pressure to say YES or move toward a sale, but rather increasingly realizes that his EQ is higher than first thought. The question is, "how little does he have to bend to do business with you now?" If this prospect entered the process through a Catch & Release system (see previous chapter), then we have an idea where the buyer feels his EQ is. It's the seller's job to keep that ever rising. Making the bend the buyer needs to make smaller and smaller.

Seller: I would guess that you are perfectly satisfied with your current situation, aren't you ("NO Selling")?

Buyer: Well, yes, I am pretty satisfied.

Seller: Pretty satisfied. Does that mean you're very satisfied, or are there issues that can be improved ("NO Selling")?

Buyer: Well, they have been late on several deliveries (fact). Can you guarantee delivery dates (EQ)?

Seller: Late (gentle)? Help me understand what happened (more detail)?

Buyer: They were four days late (again, this is fact, not EQ, but "listen" for emotion in tone and body).

Seller: Not a big problem, is it ("NO Selling")? First time they have been late?

Buyer: This is the second time (facts but "listen" for EQ tone and body language)!

Seller: So what have you done to correct it (direct)?

Buyer: Nothing; we warned them (EQ)!

Seller: After the warning they won't be late again, will they ("NO Selling")?

Buyer: They'd better not be (emotion from tone is EQ, Seller more willing to bend).

Seller: So, (very gentle) how did that impact you personally (direct)?

Buyer: (In an edgy tone of voice...getting emotional, now) I'm on the hot seat if they are late again. It's my job to get the supplies here on time (EQ).

Seller: Um, (very gentle) how are you feeling about it (direct)?

Buyer: I'm frustrated (with emotion). I did everything right and they were still late (EQ).

Seller: But...it sounds like you're not going to do anything about it (direct)?

Buyer: How is your delivery time? Do you keep your promises?

Seller: I won't promise delivery times if I know I can't make them (gentle, don't go into I-can-convince-you). What happens if we can't promise delivery when you want it every time ("NO Selling")?

... And the communication continues.

This is an example of one EQ sequence. Sometimes the sequence doesn't uncover any increase in EQ. From a Catch & Release point of view, perhaps this prospect is a "NO" and seller should move on. Sometimes the sequence is very short when the emotion is clearly expressed by the buyer and understood by the seller. Sometimes the conversation may be lengthy. This dialogue has raised the EQ, but the seller should continue to discover more EQ. Without clarifying what level of EQ the buyer has, the seller is reduced to only the basest agreement techniques....usually price.

Rule: Ask "What else?"

The seller must look for multiple issues and emotions that raise the buyer's EQ. The higher the EQ, the less the buyer has to bend and the more flexibility the seller has with offering and price. The level of EQ determines the value of the seller's offering to the buyer. EQ=$.

These dialogues are very short examples of NO Selling. Many more rules can be added to these few. These are a start.

Power-of-No Selling is powerful. It requires a change in perspective, an open mind. The psychological issues confronted in Power-of-NO Selling are either working for you or against you. The degree of mutuality between Grandpa and Elmer either improves the communication or it destroys it. The Logical Qualifiers and the Emotional Qualifiers are already there. The buyer's and seller's ability to discover and identify LQ and EQ is either improving the communication or not. LQ and EQ are not neutral. Communication techniques are working either positively or negatively for the buyer and the seller. The higher the level of awareness, the better the buyer and seller understand each other.

Power-of-NO Selling focuses attention on the NO side of the buy/sell communication – a side that traditional sellers would rather ignore. When tradin' and makin' deals, NO cannot be ignored. NO is the power, NO gives the communication integrity and NO provides free will to both the buyer and the seller.

ABOUT DAVID ALLEN

David Allen has had 10 years of training and consulting experience specializing in sales training, management training, management consulting services, executive coaching and customer service training. His St. Louis organization does business with about 60 companies and organizations and several hundred individuals in all types of selling.

David has trained thousands of people in industries from finance to construction and from high tech to traditional manufacturing. He is not afraid to challenge the traditional ways of selling and marketing products and services. He presents the "No Wimp" approach to selling in a serious, rigorous but enjoyable course.

CHAPTER XI.

Postscript:
The Two Sides of NO

Kim DeMotte

As we end this treatise on the mighty little word "no," and how using it or not using it can greatly affect outcomes of all kinds, it is important to focus on the duality of the message.

First, it is up to *you* to establish your limits, form your "red ring," publish your **Ideal Target** and take advantage of being as clear about what you don't want as you are about what you want. This alone will set you apart from your peers. It will generate clarity in all that you do. People will understand implicitly who you are by observing the courage and consistency of your limits applied to everything from sales processes to ethics to employee relations. Leadership is much easier when you are understood.

As you have seen, continuing to manage projects (be they sales, productivity, human resource, or profit based) using **Anything Goes Targets** or **Fuzzy Targets** leaves those around us (and sometimes ourselves) wondering what we really want. It takes real courage to establish a limit and give your sales team marching orders to NOT take any business with gross margins under 7%. It takes real guts to look at an applicant for a critical position that has been vacant for fourteen months and pass because the applicant doesn't have the required experience.

Second, it's up to *you* to help others determine *their* limits and use NO effectively. To do otherwise would be hypocritical. To perceive a NO when it is not the word spoken is to reach the Ph.D. level of the Positive Power of NO. The big test will come when you want so badly for someone to commit to your proposal, but you can see they're struggling to agree. Helping them say NO moves everyone toward the most successful conclusion. Your counterpart is relieved by not committing to something that was outside his limit (although he may not have realized it). And you don't end up with the inefficiencies and ineffectiveness of less-than-total commitment.

In the previous pages we trust you have seen how this premise can help you and the projects you manage. We hope you take the ideas and use them to improve at least one small aspect of your business life.

> **The Positive Power of NO is the advantage you get when you're as clear about what you DON'T want as you are about what you WANT.**
>
> **NO is the Foundation of Free Will, the Cornerstone of Character and the Icon of Integrity.**

Pass it on!

INDEX